T0649108

Entering an intimate relationship
with the
Heavenly Father...

WHEN *FATHER*
IS A
BAD WORD

DAN KUIPER

Back cover photo by Robert Linkiewicz

Copyright © 2012 Dan Kuiper

All rights reserved.

ISBN: 0988247909

ISBN 13: 9780988247901

Contents

Acknowledgments

I would like to thank several people whom God has strategically placed in my life and who have helped make this book a reality. Thanks to my biggest supporter and encourager this side of heaven, my wife, Jan, and to our children, Greg, Mindy, and Traci, who have been wonderfully patient through the years while I've tried to figure this father thing out.

Thanks to Norman LeClercq who urged me to answer God's calling, step out of the boat, and write this book. Also to Terry Top and Rich Grevengoed from New Leaf Resources whom God brought into my life at a crucial time to help me turn over a new leaf. Thanks to Bob Blahnik, my mentor and friend, who taught me the importance of being authentic in my relationships with God and others. To Laryn Zoerhof, who asked the questions that led to a quest: discovering who my Heavenly Father really is.

And thanks to my Heavenly Father who continually uses people to reveal more and more of His fatherly nature to me and who has given me the privilege of being that person for others.

Introduction

Father. For some, this word conjures up feelings of warmth, security, and pride. For all too many others, however, the word triggers shame, pain, and anger.

The relationship we have with our fathers has a profound effect on every human relationship we have on this earth. Furthermore, it plays a crucial role in shaping the relationship we have with God.

I have known firsthand the pain of growing up with an alcoholic father. Through the years I have discovered how my dad's drinking not only drove a wedge between the two of us, but also became a barrier between me and God.

I unwittingly transferred characteristics of my earthly father to my Heavenly Father, creating inadvertent distance between us. My journey toward spiritual health has led me to a profoundly more accurate understanding of my Heavenly Father. The journey has also led me to cross paths with countless people who are dealing with (or not dealing with, as the case may be) the same dilemma: adults, teens, and children whose concept of their Heavenly Father has been tainted by relationships with their earthly fathers that were far from ideal. This book is for them.

The truth of the matter is this: There is a direct parallel between how we experience our fathers and how we experience our God. The toxins from a strained or nonexistent father-child relationship can be lethal to our relationship with God. If our father's anger or abuse, or perhaps his apathy or absence, poisoned our home life, there is a strong likelihood our spiritual life will also be tainted as we experience our Heavenly Father in much the same way.

Misconceptions about God can be devastating. Seeing God as angry, distant, continually displeased, or just plain indifferent will not exactly make us long to get close to Him. The thought of getting hurt again by a father prevents the intimacy that God desires to have with His kids. We convince ourselves that it's not worth the risk. Some of us just walk away.

But the sad reality is, when we walk away from our Heavenly Father we are turning our backs on the only One who can provide healing for our father wounds.

I am no medical expert. It has come in very handy that I married a registered nurse. In our home my wife has had to deal with a variety of maladies, illnesses, and injuries, not to mention the subsequent crying, screaming, and demands to "kiss it and make it better," to which she usually responds, "Quit whining. You're worse than the kids." But watching how she operates (no pun intended) in a situation where there is blood involved, I have learned a great deal. For instance, I have been taught that there are three things that can make open wounds dangerous. If cuts and gashes are not closed in a timely manner, the results can be: (1) infection, (2) contamination, and/or (3) the wounds becoming larger.

Open father wounds are dangerous for the same reasons. When we don't experience closure to issues we have or had with our dads, we can easily become infected with a host of harmful invaders—anger, depression, a sense of worthlessness, and addictive behaviors, to name a few.

An interesting side note: Anyone with bad handwriting and an "MD" behind their name will tell you that, more often than not, it is infection that causes more long-term damage than the wound itself. Even the six-CD *How to Become a Professional Therapist* set sold on TV teaches that what we *think* is the problem is hardly ever the problem.

Unresolved issues with our dads can also lead to contamination of our relationships with others. As a result of unhealthy interactions with our fathers, we may find it difficult, perhaps even impossible, to become truly intimate with anyone. We may be afraid of rejection. We may fear being abandoned. We may tend to expect the worst in most situations. We may keep people at arm's length because of our inability to trust. We may internalize anger that erupts at the slightest provocation.

Road rage is a good example. A driver takes offense at another driver and starts screaming, hollering, and cursing, while possibly adding corresponding hand gestures. This behavior often results in altercations, assaults, and accidents.

Is an avalanche of anger justified simply because a poor schmuck in a Honda Civic failed to turn on his blinker? Is it possible there is a more deserving target? Road rage could very well have more to do with care-less fathers than with careless drivers.

In addition to infecting us and contaminating others, when we don't seek to close our father wounds quickly there is a great risk of the wounds becoming larger, causing an even greater threat to our health and well-being. Left unchecked, resentment and lack of forgiveness will continue to eat away at our insides, causing our condition to worsen.

The good news is, no matter how deep our father wounds, complete healing is possible. That healing is found in relationship with our Heavenly Father. It is an accurate understanding of Him that will soothe our wounds. It is knowing His nature that will provide balm for our hurts. It is entering into an intimate relationship with Him that will allow us to experience the love, healing, and grace He longs to give His children. In the tender care of our Heavenly Father our prognosis is excellent.

My prayer is that this book will help introduce you to a Heavenly Father you may not have known before. He is a Father we can trust; a Father who will never leave us; a Father who will love us no matter what; a Father who protects us and wants us to prosper; a Father who longs to hold us; a Father who encourages His children; a Father who genuinely wants to spend time with us and is pleased with us; a Father who suffers with us; a Father who gives us hope and a future. The solution to the problems caused by living with father wounds is developing a relationship with the Heavenly Father.

I must confess that I have been putting off writing this book for some time because I knew what was in store for me when I chose to address the subject of father issues. When I first began in ministry, my mentor gave me a warning. He cautioned that God would help me to better understand whatever topic I was preaching or teaching by making me deal with that issue in my own life. He told me that whenever God led him to preach or teach about a specific issue, he could be sure that throughout his preparation time, God would bring that issue front and center in his own life and force him to deal with it first.

His words proved prophetic. The next time I preached I spoke on the timeless topic of patience. Never in my life was my patience tested more than when I was preparing for that message. I learned my lesson. I don't preach on patience anymore. Once, my mentor asked me to fill in for him two Sunday mornings while he was on vacation. When I readily agreed he smirked and asked me what subject I wanted to preach on. I responded, "The joy of sex." I reasoned, "If I have to personally experience what I'm preaching on, it might as well be enjoyable."

My fear in writing this book was that delving into this subject matter would dredge up pain from the past that I wanted to believe had been settled. Even more, I feared that going through this process might bring about new hurts. However, as I've continued on my path toward recovery, God has revealed to me enough about His character that I can have complete confidence that good will result from whatever gets stirred up.

Before we begin this journey together please know that I do not presume to know the solutions to all of life's problems. I am not Dan the Answer Man. I am a fellow struggler who is trying to make sense of life and help others to do the same. Seeking a growing relationship with God makes sense.

CHAPTER 1

When You Hear The Word *Father*

I will be a Father to you, and you will be my
sons and daughters, says the Lord Almighty.

2 Corinthians 6:18, NIV

They were not so much questions as right hooks to the gut—well-timed queries from a well-intentioned pastor that evaded my defenses and hit me where it hurt.

Maybe his questions wouldn't pack much of a wallop for you. But for me, at this point in the match, they sent me to the canvas with cartoon birdies circling above my head. I was already wrestling daily with troublesome questions: *Why was I so depressed? Why did I wake up every morning with a nagging sense of emptiness in my soul? How could I be a Christian and yet have no peace in my life? Why did I feel like God was a million miles away? When was I going to feel normal again?*

I kept telling myself that I *should* be happy. I *should* be grateful that I had a successful business. I *should* be thrilled that I had a beautiful wife and three wonderful children. I *should* find great satisfaction from having a nice home in a pleasant neighborhood. I *should* have joy, joy, joy, joy down in my heart. But I wasn't happy or grateful or satisfied or joyful. And it didn't make sense.

Prayer Walks

I found myself taking a lot of prayer walks. I'm not really sure why I called them that. Prayer is supposed to be *communication with God,*

> **Prayer is supposed to be communication with God, and communication entails an *exchange* of information or messages.**

and communication entails *an exchange* of information or messages. Its root word, *commune,* means *to talk together intimately.* Yet my prayer walks involved neither exchanging nor communing. I was doing all the talking. There was no question and answer—only questions. And there certainly was no intimacy. But I kept walking and talking.

I had memorized many Bible verses in Sunday School when I was a child. It wasn't so much that I yearned to know the Holy Scriptures. I just wanted at least as many self-adhesive stars on the class performance chart as the other kids had. But, despite my impure motives, there were dozens of verses stored in my memory bank. One of them sprung to mind one day while on a prayer walk. I recalled that Jesus once said, "Ask, and it shall be given you; seek, and ye shall find; knock, and it shall be opened unto you: For every one that asketh receiveth; and he that seeketh findeth; and to him that knocketh it shall be opened" (Matt. 7:7–8, King James Version [KJV]).

Asking, Seeking, and Knocking

The New Living Translation (NLT) of the Bible wasn't around when I was a kid in Sunday School and had to memorize stuff Jesus said. I wish it had been. I find the NLT to be much more recite-able. The words of Jesus in the New Living Translation of Matthew 7 are, "Keep on asking, and you will receive what you ask for. Keep on seeking, and you will find. Keep on knocking, and the door will be opened to you."

Unfortunately for me, I kept on asking, but only came up with more questions. I would've made a stellar *Jeopardy* contestant because my whole life was in the form of a question. I kept on seeking, but was left feeling like a kid playing hide and seek with friends who had all returned to their homes while I was still counting to a hundred behind a tree. I kept on knocking, but no one answered the door. I wondered if God was even home. But I kept on. I wasn't sure if it was persistence or stupidity, but thankfully, I kept on asking and seeking and knocking.

The Opened Door

On one particular morning while out on a prayer walk, I noticed a lone car in the parking lot of a church down the street from my house. I didn't see a mini-Bible on the front seat or the outline of a fish affixed above the bumper, but I took a chance that the car belonged to the pastor and went inside. There was no one at the secretary's desk to act as security, so I proceeded directly to the pastor's office. There I knocked, and the door was opened. A kindly man greeted me and I asked if I could have a few moments of his time.

He invited me to sit in a faded, old, wing-backed chair opposite his mahogany L-shaped desk. To save us both some time, I gave a quick account of my problems in hopes of a quick solution. But even the Reader's Digest version of what was going on in my life made my muscles twitch. As I verbalized my troublesome questions, my words were becoming more and more emotionally charged. I needed help in diagnosing why I felt so bad when my life was so good. I needed to know why I felt so disconnected from God.

After describing my dilemma in a nutshell I wondered if the pastor thought I was a nutcase. He leaned back in his chair and put his hand to his chin. I was already feeling vulnerable and unprotected when he delivered the first of two punches that left me staggering.

3

In a soothing, gentle voice as if speaking to a baby he asked, "When you pray, how do you address God?"

Direct hit. The pain in my gut was immediate. I instinctively crossed my arms and pulled them tight across my stomach. When I caught my breath and cleared my throat, I answered haltingly, "Father."

Before I could get my bearings he delivered the back end of the one-two punch. "When you hear the word *father*, what image comes to mind?"

When I was growing up, I could never understand why whenever I would irritate my mom she would say, "Keep it up and I'll knock you into the middle of next week." But I must say this question knocked me back about twenty-five years. If there was a referee in the room, he would have thrown up his hands and called the fight. My head was spinning like a Tilt-a-Whirl. I could feel everything, yet I could feel nothing. It was painfully obvious I had an open wound, and the pastor had stuck his finger right in it.

My Story

From the time I was five years old until I was twenty-one, my father was an active, verbally abusive alcoholic. He was drunk throughout most of my childhood—his unwritten excuse for missing band concerts and ballgames, plays and parent-teacher conferences.

Dad was a religious alcoholic; he never drank on Sunday. Apparently, that wasn't the Christian thing to do. Sunday was the day our family put on our fine clothes and fake smiles and went to church pretending that, like everyone else in attendance, we had it all together. The image of our family seated on that

Sunday was the day our family put on our fine clothes and fake smiles and went to church pretending that, like everyone else in attendance, we had it all together.

wooden bench on Sunday mornings was so artificially sweet that it would have made an avowed atheist smile and nod in approval.

But Monday through Saturday were different. After work, Dad found drinking with his buddies at Alex's Tap more beneficial than having dinner with his family. On most occasions he would drink until he was drunk. If bar stools had seatbelts, he would have stayed even longer. Once he had downed at least twice the legal limit he would pay his tab, either by cash or IOU, and stagger across the parking lot in search of his truck. One night he walked (and I use that verb loosely) all the way home from Alex's. He barged through the back door muttering that someone had stolen his truck, not remembering that his truck was in the shop for repairs and he had taken the car to work that day. Whether he was driving or walking, any guardian angels assigned to my dad should have gotten time-and-a-half.

Jeckyll and Hyde

The effects of alcohol on my dad were startling. After a few beers and a couple of shots this slight, unassuming man would be transformed into a raging monster. It was truly a Dr. Jekyll and Mr. Hyde situation. And with more and more regularity the doctor was not in.

None of the homes on the block where we lived in northwest Indiana had central air conditioning. However, no matter how sticky and sultry the summer evenings were, our house was often closed up tighter than a dance floor at a Baptist wedding reception in a weak effort to prevent the neighbors from hearing Dad's alcohol-induced tirades. Dad was bilingual. He spoke one language at church on Sunday and a different language when he was

Dad was bilingual. He spoke one language at church on Sunday and a different language when he was home the rest of the week. I was unsure which was his second language.

home the rest of the week. I was unsure which was his second language.

The only silver lining in the ominous cloud that hung over our house was that Dad was not physically abusive. He never hit me, my mom, or my siblings. But his words left marks all over us—blaming, shaming, ruthless, truth-less words that many times made physical abuse seem preferable. Ironically, he often screamed at us about our "lack of respect" for him as the head of the family.

Many times, after he would fall into bed and we thought the worst was over, he would wake up, head back to the kitchen, and open the refrigerator for reinforcements. Soon, even though we thought we had already experienced the grand finale, the fireworks show would begin again. I remember, on more than one occasion, being scared awake by the sound of pots and pans being thrown across the kitchen floor by the man demanding respect.

But here's the kicker. As I sat in the pastor's office that day, Dad had been sober already for several years. God must have been listening on my earlier prayer walks, for He delivered my dad from alcoholism, restored my relationship with him, and allowed me to get to know him apart from alcohol. I discovered that when Dad wasn't drinking, he was great guy. I felt genuinely blessed to have experienced something that so many children of alcoholics never experience: a parent's sobriety. God allowed me to see my father as a kind, caring, sensitive Christian man who had also been praying for years, right along with me and the rest of the family, that he would be delivered from alcohol's grasp.

Better or Worse

God had protected my parents' marriage. Mom never suspected when she vowed to remain faithful to my dad "for better or worse" what "worse" was going to look like. I have seen marital bonds severed for far lesser offenses.

I remember a conversation I had with my mom one morning when I was about thirteen. We had just experienced another typical night in the Kuiper household. About an hour after Mom and I had our

Mom never suspected when she vowed to remain faithful to my dad "for better or worse" what "worse" was going to look like.

usual silent supper, Dad blasted through the back door.

I was in my bedroom hurriedly trying to finish my homework in the calm before the inevitable storm. My room was at the opposite end of the house from the back door. I could not see him come into the house, but I could tell in a nanosecond he was drunk. I didn't have to visualize his vacant, bloodshot eyes. I didn't need to hear the slurred speech. No breathalyzer test was required. As the child of an alcoholic, I had special training. Hypervigilance was my modus operandi. My senses—all six of them—were always on full-scale alert. I could tell with dead-on accuracy if Dad was intoxicated simply by listening as he climbed the three steps on our back landing. If his steps were uneven or I detected the sound of his metal lunchbox scraping the plaster wall, I knew that he had spent too long at Alex's and I would immediately begin bracing myself for another long and terrifying night. This was one of those nights.

Dad stumbled to the kitchen table and began eating the dinner Mom had set aside for him. The war began, as it usually did, with a single shot. "Why is my food cold?" The only thing I could be more sure of than Dad baiting my mom was Mom taking the bait—hook, line, and sinker.

"Your food wouldn't be cold if you came home on time to have supper with your family instead of drinking with your so-called friends." And so it began.

For Dad it was an all-too-common night of screaming, cursing, outrageous accusations, drinking more beer, and denying he had a drinking problem. For my mom and me, it was a night of tears, fears, drinking Maalox, and wondering when the drinking problem he denied he had would ever end.

The morning after this particular tumultuous night, when my mom and I were alone in the kitchen, I, in a moment of weakness, broke family rule number one: *Don't ever talk about "the problem."* I blurted out, "I can't take any more of this. If he wants to ruin his life let him, but he can't drag you and me down with him. It's time you get a divorce."

My mother's response was calm, yet firm: "I made a vow to your father and to God, and I'm not going to break it." God blessed my mother with a strong sense of commitment. That's the Christian way of saying she was incredibly stubborn. But whatever you call it, it kept their marriage and our family together.

Images

As I sat in the pastor's office, I had been telling myself for months that I had no right to feel down. My prayers had been answered. God had granted Dad sobriety. That harrowing chapter of our lives was not only over, but it had a happy ending. And yet it was a simple follow-up question from a discerning pastor that made me realize that even though Dad's drinking days were over, the traumatic effects of his alcoholic behavior lived on.

I tried to swallow, but my Adam's apple was the size of a red Jonathon. I repeated, "What image comes to mind when I hear the word *father?*" I started, "A father is…" Once I got those first three words out, my response gushed like errant fire hose. "A father is someone who I can't trust he is someone who is never there when I need him he is someone who says he loves me but doesn't ever show it he is someone I'm afraid of he is someone who has no regard for my feelings he is someone who never compliments me but is quick to criticize he is someone who chooses not to spend time with me he is someone I can't get close to he is someone who I cannot possibly please."

After years of holding a tight rein on my emotions here I was emoting all over the place. I wiped the tears from my face—as best I could with sweaty palms—and looked up, half expecting to find the pastor taking shelter behind the desk. Instead, he was leaning toward me and, with a warm smile lighting his face, he said, "I'm not sure I'd want to pray to a God like that."

Yet that is exactly the God to whom I had been praying. As an adult I was viewing my Heavenly Father the same way I, as a child, viewed my earthly father. No wonder we weren't bonding.

> **As an adult I was viewing my Heavenly Father the same way I, as a child, viewed my earthly father. No wonder we weren't bonding.**

Fallout

The familial and societal fallout from unhealthy father-child relationships irradiates our land. A national survey conducted in 1999 by the Gallup Organization for the National Center for Fathering showed that 72.2 percent of those polled agreed that "the physical absence of the father from the home is the most significant problem facing America."

Most of us are aware that the relationship a child has with his or her father is fundamentally important to his or her development. While much attention has been given in our society to the mother-child relationship, research has shown that the relationship between fathers and their children is significantly more important to children's overall development than previously believed:

- Having a loving and nurturing father is as important for a child's happiness, well-being, and social and academic success as having a loving and nurturing mother.[1]

- "Children with an involved father are exposed to more varied social experiences and are more intellectually advanced

9

than those who only have regular contact with their mother. Infants with two involved parents can cope better with being alone with strangers and also seem to attend more effectively to novel and complex stimuli. Well-fathered children have a greater breadth of positive social experiences than those exclusively reared by their mothers."[2]

- "Children with involved, loving fathers are significantly more likely to do well in school, have healthy self-esteem, exhibit empathy and pro-social behavior, and avoid high-risk behaviors such as drug use, truancy, and criminal activity compared to children who have uninvolved fathers."[3]

- "For the children of non-resident fathers, negative changes in the parent-child relationship were the best predictor of a child's internalizing (depression, etc.) and externalizing (violence) behaviors."[4]

- Disruption of the family during childhood, including the lack of a father's involvement, increases the odds that a child will engage in antisocial behaviors such as fighting, lying, cheating, and criminal activity.[5]

- "Boys with absent fathers are statistically more likely to be violent, get hurt, get into trouble, do poorly in school and be members of teenage gangs in adolescence. Fatherless daughters are more likely to have low self-esteem, to have sex before they really want to, get pregnant, be assaulted and not continue their schooling."[6]

- An increased amount of father-child involvement has proven to increase a child's social stability, educational achievement, and even his or her potential to have a solid marriage as an adult. The children are also more curious about the world around them and develop greater problem solving skills.[7]

Hats off to single moms. No job is more difficult. But the cold, stark reality is this: A mom can be a nurturer, an encourager, a counselor, a mentor, even a bread-winner, but she can never be a father.

Fathers shape us physically, emotionally, intellectually, socially, psychologically, economically, behaviorally, and relationally. However, our father's effect on us spiritually has the most severe consequences. Moreover, the spiritual consequences of a father's involvement (or lack thereof) in the lives of his children are not simply long-term; they are eternal.

The relationship a child has with his or her father has a profound impact on the relationship, if any, she or he has with God. It is normal even for those who are raised in a healthy family system to project significant people in their lives onto others and expect them to behave in similar ways. It is common to project our parents onto teachers, bosses, spouses—even God. In the world of psychology this is known as transference.

> **The relationship a child has with his or her father has a profound impact on the relationship, if any, she or he has with God.**

It is very typical for children and adults to project their dads onto God. For some, that can be a good thing. For others, it can be very, very bad.

- Boys whose dads walked out on the family often grow up to be men who believe they can't rely on God. They rationalize, "Why trust Him? He'll just walk one day, too."

- Daughters of workaholic dads can become women with an insatiable need to be noticed and feel close to God, but who are often left disappointed. They attribute their earthly father's voice to their Heavenly Father: "Not now. I'm busy."

- Sons of strict, legalistic, judgmental dads often, in their adult life, view God as someone whose love must be earned. Their spiritual life—like their home life—is all about following the rules.

- Girls who were sexually abused by their fathers become, in many cases, women who find they simply cannot have a close relationship with a male God. The word *intimacy* for them has been ruined forever.

Here is the dilemma: When we have significant father issues and transfer them onto our Heavenly Father, we build a wall between us and Him. In doing so, we separate ourselves from precisely what we're looking for—a growing, trusting, loving, saving relationship with a Father who truly wants what's best for His kids.

Even though the concept I had of my Heavenly Father was based on my earthly father experience I hoped beyond hope that somehow my Heavenly Father was different. An impromptu counseling session with an insightful pastor propelled me to find out if He was.

As I sat that day in the pastor's office it was clear that I had some unfinished business in my life that needed to be finished. I still lacked peace in my spirit. I continued to be held captive by irrational fears. I needed healing for my still wounded soul. But before I could find what I was looking for, something needed to happen first: I needed to discover who my Heavenly Father really was.

CHAPTER 2

A Father We Can Trust

We're never so vulnerable as when we trust someone—but paradoxically, if we cannot trust, neither can we find love or joy.

Walter Anderson

Paula came from a seemingly perfect family. If you saw their picture in the pictorial church directory, you would want to Photoshop yourself into it. Paula's dad was one of those people who never had a hair out of place—whether he was singing in the church choir or bagging leaves in his front lawn. He was conscientious—a hard worker who provided well for the family.

When she was in high school, Paula's parents were leaders of her church youth group. Paula's friends adored her parents, especially her dad. Whenever he wasn't away on business he served as the unofficial chaplain of Paula's tennis team. He would lead the team in prayer before they would compete. Paula's friends characterized him as "awesome," "nice," and "easy to talk to." Anyone who spent any amount of time around Paula's family, including Paula herself, would tell you that her mom and dad had an ideal marriage.

But then came that dreadful day. Paula refers to it as "the day when my life as I knew it ended."

Paula had come home from school to find an official-looking black car with heavily tinted windows parked in the driveway. She walked into the living room to find two men in dark suits seated on the couch. Her mother sat across from them in a chair, her hand over her mouth, her cheeks streaked with tears.

"I will never forget that scene," Paula recounted. "Mom looked up at me, covered her face with her hands, and began sobbing. I just ran to her and hugged her. One of the men said, 'We'll be going now. I'll leave my card on the counter. If you have any further questions, give me a call.'"

"Mom, what's going on?" Paula asked after hearing the front door close.

The words that were about to come from her mother's mouth would change Paula's life forever. "Your father's in jail."

That statement was so far out of the realm of Paula's comprehension that she needed to be persuaded it was true. While the two of them finished off an entire box of Kleenex, Paula's mom explained to her how her father had been arrested for embezzling thousands of dollars from his employers over a period of several years. But the news got worse. The federal investigation also revealed that when her father was away on business, he was often in the company of disreputable women.

Paula stood straight, defied her tears, and said, emphatically, as if trying to convince herself, "Not Dad." "When did...," Paula began. "Why... How could..." Her sentences were as broken as her heart.

In the years that followed, Paula had to come to terms with her father's trial, imprisonment, and subsequent release—each of which came with its own brand of anguish. Then there was the divorce.

It's a shame that the word *grief* is almost always associated with death because all significant losses need to be grieved.

It's a shame that the word *grief* is almost always associated with death because all significant losses need to be grieved. Paula needed to grieve the loss of her parents' marriage. What's more, she needed to grieve the loss of an ideal. She lost a way of life. She lost a relationship with the father she thought she knew. But, perhaps the most destructive loss in Paula's life: She had lost the ability to trust.

One Sunday morning, some twenty years after her father's secret life was brought to light, Paula, still single, found herself sitting in a church many miles from the one her father took her to as a child. She sat alone in a church congregation of three hundred.

Since the day of her father's arrest, it seemed as if Paula's life was in a constant state of upheaval. It was as if Paula's emotions were off-roading in a school bus. Medication only provided a loosely fitting restraint. Paula came to the realization that she needed more peace than Xanax could provide. While, in a self-protective move, she had distanced herself from the God her father had so openly professed, she couldn't deny her deep-seated belief that God could provide what she needed.

Paula couldn't remember much of the sermon that morning. As the preacher preached on she was still replaying the words of Jesus he quoted in his opening blessing: "Peace I leave with you; my peace I give you. I do not give to you as the world gives. Do not let your hearts be troubled and do not be afraid" (John 14:27, New International Version [NIV]).

That was the kind of peace she needed. Not the kind the world gives—peace that is manufactured in cans, cartons, and capsules. She needed that peace from God that she heard about as a little girl as she sat in the pew next to her father, peace *which passeth all understanding* (Phil. 4:7, KJV).

After daydreaming about that peace throughout the pastor's message Paula was shocked back into reality when he offered this conclusion: "The level of peace we experience in our lives is determined by the level of trust we place in our Heavenly Father." Paula immediately came to her own conclusion. If the kind of peace she was looking for was dependent upon trusting a Father, she would just have to learn to live without it.

Trust, indeed, can be very dangerous because trust depends on vulnerability. And vulnerability always carries risk.

In this journey called life I have come across all kinds of people—children, teens, and adults—who have, for very good reasons, found it difficult or downright impossible to trust their fathers. One would like to believe that it is an inalienable right for children to be able to trust the very one who gave them life. Yet countless people bear the bruises of having trusted their fathers only to be left disappointed, dejected, and disillusioned. The heartache that results from a father's broken trust makes it infinitely more risky to trust anyone—our Heavenly Father included.

> **Trust, indeed, can be very dangerous because trust depends on vulnerability. And vulnerability always carries risk.**

Hopeful Expectation

Brian was so excited he hardly slept. He got out of bed, put on his pinstriped Mets jersey and cap, grabbed the baseball glove he had slept with, and bounced into the kitchen. Today was the day his dad was taking him to his first major league baseball game.

Brian's dad worked a lot of hours causing untoward tension between husband and wife and father and son. When Brian's Boy Scout troop went on their father-son outing to a Mets game, his dad canceled at the last minute. Some work obligation came up. Brian, not wanting to be the only boy without a dad, chose to stay home. But all that was forgiven now. Brian and his dad were going to a game.

When he entered the kitchen Brian immediately scanned the room. For much of his young life, Brian's radar was on full-scale alert as he looked and listened for verbal and non-verbal cues that might signal the end of his parents' marriage. Through most of his nine years, he operated under a minimum threat level of orange. His mom was standing at the kitchen sink rinsing dishes. "Where's Dad?" Brian asked.

"He had to go into the office for a couple of hours." Brian's face fell as his heart sank. "But he said he'd be home by noon to pick you up," she quickly added.

Brian beamed and bounded out the door. Brian didn't have much opportunity to spend time with his dad, just the two of them. His dad had started a new business and routinely worked seventy to eighty hours a week. Their conversations mostly consisted of Brian saying "good night" on those rare occasions when his dad came home before Brian's bedtime. But this day Brian and his dad were going to a game.

Brian stood in the front lawn throwing himself pop-ups, dreaming of being a big league player with his dad in the stands cheering him on, telling everyone within hearing distance, "That's my boy."

Brian alternately looked at the baseball, his watch, and the street, praying that he would soon see his dad's car approaching. When he first checked the time it was eleven o'clock. By noon Brian began to get that pain in the pit of his stomach again.

"Come on, Dad," he said to himself. "I don't want to be late.

Broken Promises

At 12:15 p.m. Brian dropped his baseball glove and went into the house. His mom's worried expression mirrored his. "I'm sure he's just hung up in traffic," she reasoned. Brian hoped that's all it was. But history told him otherwise. Plans for picnics, camping trips—even family vacations—were often scrapped as Dad's almighty schedule was deemed more important.

Just then, Brian heard a car door slam. Dad was home! He flew out the door, scooped up his glove, and made it to the car in roughly six seconds flat. "Hey, Dad! You ready to go?" Before Brian could open the passenger door, his father put his hands on his son's shoulders.

"Brian, I'm sorry. I'm going to have to give you a rain check on the game today."

Brian's chest deflated. "You promised," he panted, trying to hold his tears at bay.

"I know, I know. But I totally forgot about a business appointment I made for this afternoon. We'll go next Saturday."

"There is no game next Saturday," Brian seethed without separating his teeth.

"Then we'll go the next week," his father offered. Brian didn't buy it. He pulled away from his father's grasp, threw his glove against the car, and ran into the house. As he retreated to his bedroom, his mother went outside to begin damage control.

The conversation his parents had in the driveway continued to escalate to the point where Brian could hear them arguing from his room. He couldn't hear words, just emotions. After a couple of minutes the slamming of the back door signaled the end of the fight. Either it was Dad coming in to tell Brian to get his butt out to the car so they could go to the game or it was Mom venting her disgust at her husband breaking yet another promise to their son.

Although he could have predicted it with the accuracy of a San Diego weatherman, Brian went to peer through the blinds to see who won. But when he grabbed a handful of slats and pulled them down what he saw was more than a nine-year-old brain could process. It was a scene that has played out a million times on the stage of his mind ever since. Brian watched as his dad threw his golf clubs in the back of his car and drove off for his "business appointment."

> **Brian watched as his dad threw his golf clubs in the back of his car and drove off for his "business appointment."**

By age twenty-five, the pain in the pit of Brian's stomach had developed into ulcerative colitis. Ignoring the root cause of his floating anxiety clearly wasn't working any better for Brian as an adult as it did when he was a child. Drinking just made it worse. A perceptive friend suggested he give God a try. He invited Brian to come to church with him.

Brian's first church experience was relatively harmless. He had been checking off each of the homily's points in the outline in his bulletin as the pastor made them, and with just one to go, Brian thought he would make it through unscathed. But then came the part called "Application." The pastor gave a summary of his message about the unconditional love of God then gave an impassioned plea to those in attendance to respond by giving their heart to Him. In a time of silence provided so people could do their business with God, Brian did not, as instructed, fold his hands and bow his head. He crossed his arms and shook his head. He silently said to God, "I will give You my time. I will even give You my money. But I cannot give You my heart."

Fathers and Trust

If there was ever a relationship that needs to be saturated with trust it is the relationship between a child and his or her dad. A trusting relationship with our earthly father provides stability; it helps kids to become secure in who they are. Kids who can't trust their dads often are unstable and insecure as adults.

> **If there was ever a relationship that needs to be saturated with trust it is the relationship between a child and his or her dad.**

This instability and insecurity tends to infect to varying degrees all of our relationships, including our relationship with God. If we can't trust our earthly father, what makes us think we can trust a Heavenly Father? Who's to say our Heavenly Father won't lure us into a trusting relationship with Him only to desert us? That is not a rhetorical question. It's a question that can be answered. The answer is our Heavenly Father. He says so. And in His Word He says so over and over again. The Bible paints a vivid picture of a Heavenly Father who loves His kids implicitly, who always keeps His promises, who will never betray His children's trust.

God's desire for all of His children, but especially those of us who never felt stable or secure in our relationship with our earthly father, is that we experience stability and security in our relationship with our Heavenly Father.

T-R-U-S-T

I don't often utilize acrostics. Trying to make concepts fit because they happen to start with the appropriate letter of the alphabet is like putting together a jigsaw puzzle with a hammer. That being said, I would like to offer an acrostic here that does fit. Following are five keys to unlocking our ability to trust our Heavenly Father, the first letters of which happen to spell the word *trust*. I hope you're impressed.

For us to fully trust God we must:

T alk with Him
R isk being vulnerable
U nderstand who He is
S ubmit to His will
T hank Him for His love

Talk with Him

The first step in learning how to trust our Heavenly Father is to talk with Him. This is commonly called prayer. Prayer is, very simply, talking with God. And what makes our prayers effective is talking from the heart.

The most crucial component in our conversations with God is honesty. Our Heavenly Father desires that we be honest about what is going on inside of us. He knows the feelings that are present in our hearts anyway. He wants us to be truthful about them. David, in Psalm 51, clearly understood this when he prayed to God, "Surely you desire truth in the inner parts" (Ps. 51:6, NIV).

David is one of my favorite biblical heroes; he was one of God's favorites, too. The Bible includes story after story of men and women who showed incredible faithfulness and devotion to God, with whom He had relationships that were quite special. But perhaps the greatest compliment God could ever pay a human being was bestowed upon David. God called him "a man after my own heart" (Acts 13:22, NIV).

Why such a magnanimous accolade? What was it about David that earned him this king-sized compliment? Let's check out his personality profile.

Scripture tells us that David cared for lambs, wrote poetry, and sang songs in the meadows. But don't categorize him as one of those flower-child types: warm and fuzzy, free-spirited, and overly sensitive. (If you are an animal-loving, poetry-writing musician and find that characterization offensive, maybe you shouldn't be so sensitive!)

Despite his gentle side, David was also a great warrior who accomplished some amazing feats. He battled kings and captured cities. He took on giants and lions and bears (oh, my!).

In addition to his gentle and strong sides, David also had a dark side. He was a voyeur. He was an adulterer. He had a man killed to protect his reputation. He was a crappy father.

So what on earth was it about this man that made him a man after God's own heart? I believe it comes down to one character trait. David stood out because he was brutally, refreshingly honest in his relationship with God.

The second book of Samuel describes how after David slept with Bathsheba and then had her husband killed in an attempted

David stood out because he was brutally, refreshingly honest in his relationship with God.

cover-up, God sent the prophet Nathan to David to confront him with his sin. A man's man would have denied the accusations, blamed someone else, or simply had Nathan bumped off like David did his girlfriend's husband. But David was not a man's man. David was God's man. "Then David said to Nathan, 'I have sinned against the LORD'" (2 Samuel 12:13, NIV).

David was totally honest about what was going on inside himself. There was no sugar coating, glossing over, or covering up. David was transparent. If he was wrong about something, he confessed it. If he was angry with someone, he acknowledged it. If he was afraid of something, he admitted it.

In Psalm 13 we find a rather pointed conversation David has with God in which he is wide open about what is going on in his inner part. His fear and frustration with life have taken the forefront. He is not exactly feeling warm fuzzies, assured that God is holding him close. He is feeling abandoned. "How long, O LORD? Will you forget me forever? How long will you hide your face from me? How long must I wrestle with my thoughts and every day have sorrow in my heart? How long will my enemy triumph over me?" (Ps. 13:1–2, NIV)

I find great solace in knowing that God wants to hear this kind of honesty when we talk with Him. That's because so many of my prayers sound like this.

If we are feeling forgotten by God; if we are wondering if He even notices what's going on in our life, let alone cares; if we are upset that we must deal with so much anguish and sorrow on this earth, God wants us to tell Him. He wants us to verbalize what He sees in our heart. It serves no purpose to flaunt flowery, King James Version prayers before God when the words of our mouth don't match the feelings in our heart. That memorable line from *A Few Good Men* does not apply to God. God can handle the truth.

God can handle the truth. ❙

It's also important when we talk with God to know that it is permissible to ask the question, *why?* There are many well-known phrases that people think are found in the Bible that aren't:

Spare the rod, spoil the child.

Pride goes before a fall.

Cleanliness is next to godliness.

Money is the root of all evil.

If you're not Dutch, you're not much.

Look for yourself. They're not there. Neither is the phrase *ours is not to question why.*

What David is really asking over and over again in Psalm 13 is "why," and for good reason. This psalm was more than likely written by David when he was on the run from King Saul. God had promised David that one day he would sit on the throne of Israel, but Saul had other ideas about where David could sit. David was good. Saul was bad. Yet, even though he was promised the throne by none other than God Himself, David is left trying to hold a stiff upper lip while it appeared Saul had the upper hand.

So David has a little talk with God. *Why do you keep ignoring me? Why is this happening? Why is the bad guy winning? Why can't I just be king now?*

David's inner part was a tempest of fear, frustration, anger, and betrayal. In talking with God, David got those feelings out. David expressed, in no uncertain terms, how he felt about being in that situation. But then David moves on from what he *feels* to what he *believes*. David begins the psalm with the question, "will you forget me forever?" and ends with the statement, "but I trust in your unfailing love; my heart rejoices in your salvation. I will sing the LORD's praise, for he has been good to me" (Ps. 13:5–6, NIV).

David may have *felt* abandoned, but he *believed* that God was, in actuality, holding him close. He may have *felt* that God didn't care, but he *believed* that his Heavenly Father loved him. He may have *felt* that life was bad, but he *believed* that God was good. He may have *felt* that God had betrayed him, but he *believed* that God was worthy of his trust.

The first step in developing a trusting relationship with our Heavenly Father is to talk honestly with Him, especially when we are faced with difficulties in life.

As a father myself, I love it when my grown kids still call me to tell me about their day or come to me and ask, "What do think?" or "What should I do?" or "Why is this happening?" It shows how much they love and trust me.

The same is true in our relationship with our Heavenly Father. He wants us to talk to Him about everything that's going on in our lives—the good, the bad, and the ugly. He wants us to share with Him what makes us tick and what makes us ticked. If it matters to us, it matters to God.

In those times when we're overwhelmed by adversity, we need not be afraid to ask Him why awful things seem to keep coming our way. We must share with Him how we feel. We must tell Him if we are sad or lonely or hurt or scared or angry—even if our anger is directed at Him. He's God. He can handle our anger. He desires truth.

Risk Being Vulnerable

The second key to learning how to trust God is to risk being vulnerable.

When I worked in schools as a drug and alcohol abuse preventionist, I would often use the trust fall exercise with students. A trust fall is where a blindfolded person proves that he or she trusts his or her peers by falling backward into their arms.

You can learn a lot about people by watching them do this exercise. Their response is indicative of their level of trust. Some people trust fearlessly. These are the ones who fall straight back with no hesitation. Some *want* to trust, but they're just not sure they can. These are the people who kind of feel around behind them first just to be certain that there are, in fact, people there to catch them. Others are willing to trust *some*, but not completely. They are the ones who crouch down so they are closer to the floor. That way, if their fears are realized and there is no one there to catch them, it won't hurt as badly as if they were standing straight and trusting completely.

I remember doing the trust fall exercise during a classroom presentation for third graders. I didn't tell them what we were going to do. I said I needed a volunteer and almost everyone's hand went up (the single biggest difference between a group of third graders and a group of adults). I chose a bold, borderline brazen, little blonde girl. When she came forward I put a blindfold on her and asked several of her classmates to stand behind her and lock hands. I then explained to her that this was an exercise in trust.

I asked, "Do you trust me?"

She answered with a firm "Yes."

I asked, "Do you really trust me?"

"Yes," she repeated.

I said, "Great. Your classmates are right behind you. They will catch you. All you need to do is fall backward at the count of three."

Before I could even count "one," she took off the blindfold, shoved it into my chest, and said, "Do you think I'm nuts?"

Think for a moment about your earthly father. Do you trust him? Do you really trust him? For many, the answer we give in reference to our earthly father is the same response we give our Heavenly Father when He asks, "Do you trust me? Do you really trust me?"

If we are blessed to have an unshakable confidence in our earthly father because he has proven himself trustworthy, we are much more inclined to trust our Heavenly Father with that same confidence. We are more apt to fearlessly put our life in His hands, completely confident that God, like our dad, has our best interests in mind and will always catch us when we fall.

Some of us had fathers who weren't always present for us. Even if our dads were *there*, they may not have been *present*. Now, we've discovered that though we really want to trust God, we first need to be sure of His presence. We need to reach out and touch Him to know for sure that He's actually there before we trust Him with our lives.

Still others of us find that our fathers could be trusted sometimes but not all the time. They could be trusted in some areas but not others. Or, especially in the case of alcoholic or addicted fathers, they could be trusted some days but not every day. Those of us whose dads have betrayed our trust in the past often discover that we are *somewhat* trusting of God, but that we cannot consistently trust Him. We may trust Him when things are going smoothly, but not when the road gets rough.

Then there are those of us who find trusting our Heavenly Father with any part of our life simply too difficult to do. We've fallen to the ground too many times because our fathers weren't there to catch us. We've trusted our fathers because we wanted to believe that they were worthy of trust only to have our hearts broken, and we simply aren't willing to risk getting hurt again. Cognitively, we may believe that God is a Father who loves us and even that He wants good things for us, but we are unable to trust Him at an emotional level. That's the sticking point when dealing with emotions: More often than not, what we *feel* trumps what we *believe*.

More often than not, what we *feel* trumps what we *believe*. The reality is we cannot have a trusting relationship with God, or anyone for that matter, if we are not willing to risk being vulnerable. But there is a component of vulnerability that stops us dead in our tracks. Vulnerability involves surrender.

Even the most devout, spirit-filled Christians struggle with surrender. I am convinced that no matter what the congregation or denomination, when people join together to sing "I Surrender All," most of them are lying. Even singing "I Surrender Most" would be a stretch. Singing "I Surrender Some" would be much more truthful.

The truth is, God's desire is not that we surrender *some* or even *most*. He wants us to surrender *all*. God wants to be Lord of *all* in our life. Not Lord of *some*. Not Lord of *most*. Lord of *all*. It is said that if God is not Lord *of* all, He is not Lord *at* all. His desire is that we put Him squarely in charge of every aspect of our lives—our feelings and our finances, our safety and our sexuality, our doubts and our diet, our intellect and our entertainment choices.

The word *surrender* is most often defined as giving up. The very thought of giving up can trigger all kinds of fear and anxiety in people. Consider, for example, those wounded souls who were sexually victimizedby their fathers. They may have already concluded that if trusting their Heavenly Father involves surrender, that is simply too high a price to pay. But surrender to our Heavenly Father is not about giving up, it's about giving over. The third step of most twelve-step programs for overcoming addictive behaviors involves giving over our lives and our will to God.

> **Surrender to our Heavenly Father is not about giving up, it's about giving over.**

Surrender says, *God, I don't have the power to bring about lasting change in my life, but I believe that You do. I can't change my attitudes and behaviors, but I believe that You can. I don't know how I will ever learn to overcome my pain and anger so that I can trust again, but I believe that You know.*

For us to establish a trusting relationship with our Heavenly Father we must risk being vulnerable. We must surrender. We must give over our lives and our will to Him. But something needs to happen before we can take that risk.

Understand Who He Is

My friends can trust me with a lot of things. If needed, I can be trusted to take care of their lawns or their pets or their kids (provided they're potty trained). My friends can have complete confidence that I will keep secrets and supper dates. They can count on me to plan a party or pray for their problems. But they also know enough about me to never trust me to fix their cars. To say I'm not known for my mechanical ability is like saying Queen Elizabeth isn't known for her outrageous sense of humor.

When I was sixteen, I was on a date in my first car, a two-door, black-topped, red Ford Galaxie 500, when we experienced a flat tire. If Lauri hadn't known how to operate a jack, we would have had to walk to the theater. That would have been particularly problematic since we were going to a drive-in theater.

If my car makes noise, I turn up the radio. Ask me if it's front- or rear-wheel drive and I will answer, "Yes." I don't know my axle from a hole in the ground. Because my friends know me, they know what they can trust me with and what they can't.

We often require others to prove themselves before we are willing to take the risk of placing our trust in them. Before we can fully trust people, we need them to establish a track record of trustworthiness. We need to know their temperament and their character. We need to know who they really are.

The same applies in our relationship with God. Before we can put our complete trust in Him we need to understand exactly who He is.

I have gone to church almost every Sunday since long before I knew the difference between a narthex and a vestibule. Having heard thousands of sermons, which were then reinforced with weekly Sunday School and catechism lessons lest any syllable of the Holy Scriptures elude me, I have become familiar with the different names for God found in the Bible: Creator, Ancient of Days, Bright and Morning Star, Sun of Righteousness, Redeemer, Immanuel, King of Kings, Lord of Lords.

Each of these names gives us a better understanding of just who God is. And thanks to a divine encounter in a bus on a country road, there is now one particular name for God that is more endearing to me than any other.

I attended a small, Christian college in northwest Iowa. Actually, I'm not sure there are any other kind there. I felt guilty about leaving my mom home alone with an active, verbally abusive alcoholic. She never mentioned Dad's drinking in her letters, but she didn't have to. I knew what was going on and there was no reason to think that anything had changed. The script of Dad's life was quite predictable: He would go to the bar after work, then would come home drunk, usually after supper, and until about one o'clock in the morning would alternate sleeping, slurping down more beer, and finding fault with whoever was in the house.

Being away from home wasn't as freeing as I hoped it would be. When I packed up my belongings and headed off on my five-hundred-mile journey to college, I had unwittingly packed all the shame, anxiety, anger, and worry that Dad's drinking problems brought to our house. By my second semester, internalizing all that poison resulted in a stomach ulcer.

After spending three days in the hospital back home, I returned to campus. One Sunday night, soon after I had returned to school, the college choir of which I was a part crammed into a school bus and traveled to a church about an hour away from campus where we had been invited to sing at an evening worship service.

It was a cold, dark night as we returned to campus. If there was a moon, it was just a sliver. The bus ride was eerily quiet considering the vehicle was packed with college students. But after winding through a couple dozen miles of yawn-inducing farmland, the silence was broken by a baritone seated toward the front of the bus. He began softly singing an old hymn.

Like everyone else on the bus, I had grown up in a Protestant church and knew by heart every word of the more popular nineteenth-century hymns. I even knew the words to verse three of the old hymns, to which most song leaders had a strange aversion.

The school bus soloist was soon part of an ensemble and then a full choir offering four-part harmony. It was a song I had sung probably hundreds of times in my life, but for the first time I heard the message the songwriter had tried to convey. My emotions swelled along with the chorus and the words became increasingly difficult to sing. Soon, unable to make a sound at all, I just listened. I was grateful for the veil of darkness so my tears could remain private. They flowed freely as I finally grasped the truth of the familiar words I was hearing for the first time:

What a friend we have in Jesus, all our sins and griefs to bear!
What a privilege to carry everything to God in prayer!
Oh, what peace we often forfeit,
Oh, what needless pain we bear,
All because we do not carry everything to God in prayer.[8]

In the sanctity of a yellow school bus on a black night, the Holy Spirit enlightened me to the truth that God—whom I had already known as the Maker of Heaven and Earth, the Ruler over all, the Beginning and the End—was my *Friend*. He was a Friend who wanted a relationship with me; a Friend I could go to at any time. More to the point, He was a Friend who offered to replace my pain with His peace. The revelation given me that night on US 75 has proven to be a significant milestone in my spiritual journey. How I needed God to be my friend!

Each of the biblical names for God reveals a distinct aspect of His character that induces a different response from us. We can stand in awe of God the Creator. We can revere God the Holy One. We can honor God the King of Kings. But we can trust God our Friend.

But there's more. According to the Bible, he is even more than a friend. The book of Proverbs says He is a "friend that sticks closer than a brother" (Prov. 18:24, NIV). As we seek to discover who God really is we can't let the significance of that phrase escape us.

Most adults have discovered that our friends are not always life-long friends. Best friends in elementary school often have no relationship as adults. Our closest friends in high school many times are no more than casual acquaintances as we get older. Our friends today may not be our friends tomorrow. But our brother is always our brother. Not even geographical distance can change that biological fact. Our brother is always our brother. God is our friend

> **Our friends today may not be our friends tomorrow. But our brother is always our brother.**

and will always be our friend. Nothing can change that. Nothing.

Let's take a look at what else the Bible tells us to help us understand that our Heavenly Father is worthy of our trust:

- God is a Friend who can be trusted to be there for us when we are hurting. "The LORD is close to the brokenhearted and saves those who are crushed in spirit" (Ps. 34:18, NIV).

- God is a Friend who can be trusted to give us strength for the journey. "The LORD will guide you always; he will satisfy your needs in a sun-scorched land and will strengthen your frame. You will be like a well-watered garden, like a spring whose waters never fail" (Is. 58:11, NIV).

- God is a Friend who can be trusted to walk with us through tough times. "Even though I walk through the valley of the shadow of death, I will fear no evil, for you are with me; your rod and your staff, they comfort me" (Ps. 23:4, NIV).

- God is a Friend who can be trusted to help bear our worries and insecurities. "Cast all your anxiety on him because he cares for you" (1 Pet. 5:7, NIV).

It's this simple. If you don't trust God, you don't know Him. Allow Him to introduce Himself to you through His Word. Even as understanding the truth about your earthly father affects your ability to trust him, understanding the truth about your Heavenly Father will greatly impact your ability to give Him your trust. Ask Him to introduce Himself to you. He longs to be your Friend.

In his song, "This is Our God," Christian recording artist Chris Tomlin shares his understanding of God:

A refuge for the poor, a shelter from the storm
This is our God
He will wipe away your tears and return your wasted years
This is our God, oh, this is our God
A father to the orphan, a healer to the broken
This is our God
And He brings peace to our madness and comfort in our sadness
This is our God, oh this is our God
This is the one we have waited for
Oh, this is our God
A fountain for the thirsty, a lover for the lonely
This is our God
He brings glory to the humble and crowns for the faithful
This is our God [9]

I don't know about you, but I can trust a God like that.

Submit to His Will

When God first began leading me in my recovery process, I was a textbook codependent. The litmus test for determining codependency is when you hear the codependent jokes and you don't find them funny. For example:

Q: Why did the codependent cross the road?

A: To help the chicken make a decision.

Q: Why does a codependent buy two copies of every self-help book?

A: He buys one to read and one to pass on to someone who really needs it.

And the clincher: You know you're a codependent if you have a near-death experience and someone else's life flashes in front of your eyes.

If you're not even smiling right now you probably need to see a therapist, STAT.

When I first began seeing a counselor to sort things out in my life, I was so controlling of all aspects of life that I'm quite sure if God drove a car its bumper sticker would read: *LET GO AND LET DAN*. After my first few sessions, I made the deflating discovery that my dogged determination to control was not all that pleasing to God. He seems to think that's His job. I hadn't been that discouraged since I found out that sarcasm was not a spiritual gift.

I was trying to control my recovery the same way I tried to control everything else in my life—with more willpower. Just figure out what needs to be done and do it.

I am of Dutch persuasion. I don't know how I was persuaded to be Dutch but it happened. One of the most notable traits of us Dutchmen is our work ethic. We will do our job and do it very well. Then we will do your job and do it very well. We are very popular lab partners. But in addition to our being hardworking, we Wooden Shoes tend to be hardheaded. We don't want anything for nothing. I'm convinced that's why many Dutch people have such a hard time accepting grace. Seriously, if we can't work for it how can we really appreciate it?

Once my counselor made the connection that the bulk of my problems were related to the relationship I had with my father (which happened about three minutes into our first session), he suggested I go through the twelve steps of Al-Anon. I told him I was okay with the plan and suggested that to implement it we could knock off a step a week. That way I would be through with therapy and completely healed after three months. Clearly my counselor's work was cut out for him.

I honestly (and arrogantly) thought that if the healing of my father wounds was dependent on exerting more will power, the process wouldn't take long. I had the will to do whatever it took for the hurt to stop and the anger to go away. If there was one thing I had, it was willpower. But when it comes to making significant and lasting life changes, willpower is never enough.

My childhood pastor and an authority on alcoholism, Dr. Alexander DeJong, suggested that those who think they can overcome negative behaviors in life through sheer willpower should try it next time they have diarrhea. I hope you get the point because I'd really rather not have to explain it.

In truth, trusting our Heavenly Father *is* a matter of the will. But it's not so much exercising *our* will as it is submitting to *His.*

It is human nature to want our own way. If you need proof, just observe two toddlers in a room with one toy. Yet God's desire is that we set our will aside and submit to His will for our life. Submitting to God's will is at the heart of the Christian faith. Our level of trust in our Heavenly Father is dependent on the extent of our submission to Him.

When we submit to our Heavenly Father's will we are trusting that, as the all-knowing, all-powerful, ever-present God, He has a clear plan for our lives. While we know what we *want*, He knows what we *need*. He sees what we can't. His discernment is at an entirely different level than ours. The Bible confirms it: "As the heavens are higher than the earth, so are my ways higher than your ways and my thoughts than your thoughts" (Is. 55:9, NIV).

Submitting to God's will at times involves trusting Him even when common sense tells us not to.

Submitting to God's will at times involves trusting Him even when common sense tells us not to. Solomon, in his day, was the wisest man on earth. Yet he wasn't too proud to admit that he could not depend upon his reason and logic to guide him through life. He encouraged believers in the book of Proverbs, "Trust in the

Lord with all your heart and lean not on your own understanding; in all your ways submit to him, and he will make your paths straight" (Prov. 3:5–6, NIV).

To trust God fully we need to let go. We must hand the controls over to Him. We need to consciously set aside our will and submit to His. Picture yourself and God riding on a tandem bicycle. If your initial image of that has you in the front seat you've got some control issues that need to be dealt with. God wants to occupy the first seat so He can steer. Your job is to help Him pedal. He also wants you to keep your mitts off his handlebars and hold onto the ones in front of the back seat. Did you ever notice you can't steer with those? Their sole purpose is to keep you in your seat. This is a picture of submission.

There will be times we don't understand God; when we can't for the life of us figure out why certain things are happening. He wants us to trust Him anyway. It's true that it's easier to land a plane when skies are clear than when there is no visibility. But if the pilot trusts the person in the control tower, it doesn't matter if he can't even see the instrument panel, the plane can still be landed safely.

Several years ago when Jan and I were first faced with the prospect of losing her dad to cancer we found it difficult to pray, "Thy will be done." We feared what God's will might be. But our Heavenly Father, in His mercy, brought us to a point where we could finally say, "God, we don't want to give him up. We would like him healed. But we're going to put our will aside and submit to yours."

Submitting our will to God certainly isn't easy. I find great comfort in knowing that my Friend and Brother Jesus struggled with this very issue. In the Garden of Gethsemane, Jesus looked reality in the face. As the Son of God, He knew all things. He knew the time would soon come when He would be arrested and sentenced to death. Steel spikes would be driven through His hands and feet. He would die an agonizing death.

The gospels tell us that, while in the Garden of Gethsemane before His death, Jesus was filled with such extreme anguish and sorrow that His sweat was like drops of blood falling to the ground. He pleaded with God. "'Abba Father,' he cried out. 'Everything is possible for you. Please take this cup of suffering away from me.'" Jesus was none too excited about God's plan. He did not want to die. But he went on to pray, "'Yet I want your will to be done, not mine'" (Mk. 14:36, NLT). Jesus set aside His will and submitted to the will of His trustworthy Father. I, for one, am so glad He did.

Thank Him for His Love

The final key to learning how to trust our Heavenly Father is to thank Him for His love. A thankful heart finds it easier to trust.

A thankful heart finds it easier to trust.

A new role was recently added to my job description—grandfather. Although I wasn't enamored with the idea at first, reasoning that I was much too young to have a grandchild, I must admit that I've taken to it pretty well. Truth be known, the first time I held my newborn grandson close to my chest he stole my heart. There are no words to describe the depth of pride, joy, and love I felt when I first hugged that blond-haired, blue-eyed, little guy. And the thing is, he hadn't done one thing to deserve it. All he did at that point was eat and poop. Still, I loved him and continue to love him so much I would give my life for him.

Our God feels the same way when he looks at us. He takes pride in us not because of our accomplishments but because we belong to Him. Our mere existence gives Him joy. His incredible love for us is proven in that He was not only *willing* to give up His life for us, He *did*.

Because our Heavenly Father loves us as He does He gives us gifts every day, including the day itself. Bishop T.D. Jakes is fond of saying, "Each day is God's gift to you. What you do with it is your gift to Him." The greatest gift we can give Him is our gratitude.

Expressing thankfulness to our Heavenly Father, even for the seemingly insignificant things that we often take for granted, better equips us to trust Him to care for us.

So what are you thankful for? Maybe you need to start a list. The more specific you are, the deeper your level of appreciation will be.

My list includes: spending time in my perennial garden, resplendent with colors there aren't even names for, serenaded by the waterfall spilling into my pond; experiencing "goose bumps" when I feel God's breath on my neck as I worship Him in song, whether it be with thousands of people or just the two of us; going to the theater with my family for our traditional Christmas Day movie and feasting on real popcorn doused with fake butter as if we hadn't just polished off an entire ham; relaxing on a snowy day in a La-Z-Boy positioned in front of a toasty fireplace while eating M&Ms with peanuts, made not with dark chocolate, but with milk chocolate as God intended; walking barefoot along Indiana's sand dunes, hand in hand with my wife, watching the sun sink into Lake Michigan.

For the sake of marital harmony, I should clarify that these gifts are not listed in any particular order. But all are gifts from a loving Heavenly Father. Our ability to trust in Him is strengthened when we recognize, as James did in the New Testament, that "every good and perfect gift is from above" (James 1:17, NIV). But our trust in the Heavenly Father is taken to a whole new level when we reflect on the gifts He gives us in the difficult times of life; those times that, were we actually in control, we never would have gone through.

It is God's desire that we be "thankful in all circumstances" (1 Thess. 5:18). That is not to say that we are to be thankful *for* all circumstances. We're to be thankful *in* all circumstances. Our Heavenly Father best proves His trustworthiness in the negative, often agonizing experiences of life.

How I wish God would use positive circumstances in my life to bring about positive change. But since He made us, He knows our nature. We grow the most in times

We grow the most in times of difficulty and pain. of difficulty and pain. We are best refined by going through fire.

I can state with certainty that were it not for growing up in an abusive, addictive environment I would not be the person I am today. God used that particularly painful time in my life to fortify my faith, to develop my discernment, to strengthen my sense of justice, to create in me a compassionate heart—and all to levels I otherwise would never have attained. It was in the worst times of my life that God gave His best gifts. All have helped me to trust Him more.

Actually, I want to add one more item to my gratitude list. If I were ranking them this would be at the top of my list. I am grateful that my story of growing up with an alcoholic father has a happy ending. After years of prayers, God delivered my dad from drinking and allowed me to reconcile with him, for which I will be eternally grateful.

I find myself reluctant to share this news with others who have or had a similar background. It isn't because I am not thrilled beyond belief that my prayers were answered, but because I don't want to hold up a parent's recovery as the gateway to happiness. For one thing, that is a gift that many people with stories that resemble mine may never receive. But, more importantly, if we base our happiness on the behavior of others it will continue to elude us.

The goal for those of us dealing with dysfunctional dads must not be our father's recovery, but our own. It is *our* healing that leads to happiness. And that healing is not dependent on our earthly fathers. It is dependent on our Heavenly Father.

Whether or not we ever resolve our dad issues, those of us who believe can rest assured that we are fully reconciled in our relationship with God. Our Brother, Jesus, came into the world to remove all barriers between the Heavenly Father and His children. Through

Christ's death and resurrection all that is wrong between us and our Father in Heaven has been made right. In our restored relationship with Him, chaos and strife, guilt and shame, resentment and regret become things of the past. In our new relationship, the Heavenly Father offers to fill our hearts with peace that exceeds our comprehension, joy that surpasses our pain, and love that reaches beyond our circumstances. There is nothing for which I am more thankful. He has convinced me. I can trust Him in all things.

Our experiencing the fullness of life is not contingent on anything our earthly fathers may or may not do. We are filled to overflowing when we grasp what our Heavenly Father has already done. When we habitually say thank you to our Heavenly Father for all the ways He has shown His love for us, it becomes much easier to trust Him with our lives.

Talk with Him. Risk being vulnerable. Understand who He is. Submit to His will. Thank Him for His love. We need never fear our trust being betrayed by this Father.

CHAPTER 3

A Father Who Will Never Leave Us

*I look behind me and you're there, then up ahead and you're
there, too—your reassuring presence, coming and going.*

Psalm 139:5, The Message

A person's last words can tell us a lot about them. Their values, their
fears, their attitudes, and their angst often rise to the surface when
people know they are about to leave this life.

In the book *Last Words of Notable People*, William B. Brahms documents these dying utterances:

- "This is the last of earth! I am content."—President John
  Quincy Adams

- "How were the receipts today at Madison Square Garden?"—
  Entrepreneur P. T. Barnum

- "Die? I should say not, dear fellow. No Barrymore would
  allow such a conventional thing to happen to him."—Actor
  John Barrymore

- "I have tried so hard to do the right."—President Grover
  Cleveland

- "This is no time to make new enemies."—Philosopher Voltaire when asked on his deathbed to renounce Satan

- "Drink to me."—Artist Pablo Picasso

- "Damn it . . . Don't you dare ask God to help me."—Actress Joan Crawford to her housekeeper, who had begun to pray aloud.

- "All my possessions for a moment of time."—Queen Elizabeth I

The last dialogue we have with people is saved in our memories. Their final words will either be prominently displayed on the mantle of our mind or stuffed in a box and kept in a secret place. Those words, whether comforting or haunting, remain with us forever.

Separated By Death

Claire found this out at a young age. Although she was only eight years old at the time, what proved to be the last words her father spoke to her are firmly embedded in her memory. Like he did every morning when he left for work, he snuck up behind her at the breakfast table while she was munching on her Cheerios, kissed her on top of the head, gave her pony tail a playful tug, and said, "Love you, Claire Bear. Miss me, okay?"

In one of those inexplicable tragedies of life, Claire's dad, a carb-conscious, exercise-obsessed specimen of health, died at age thirty-one, a victim of a heart defect no one knew he had. He was found by a coworker with his head on his desk, next to the framed, glitter-sprinkled, macaroni masterpiece Claire had proudly presented him on Father's Day the week before.

Claire was an only child—a daddy's girl forced to grow up without a daddy. Even though Claire's mom did what moms often try to do in that situation, she couldn't possibly be both a mom *and* a dad to her daughter. Claire had a daddy-shaped hole inside her that her mother could never fill.

Her dad's last words ricocheted in her mind. Not that she needed his inadvertent reminder to miss him. She missed him every time she ate her morning cereal across from his empty chair—the empty chair that solemnified every birthday party, band concert, and ballet recital. Family celebrations, which once brought unrestrained joy, were now shrouded in black.

Claire, at thirty-one years old, provides compelling evidence that time alone does not

> **Claire had a daddy-shaped hole inside her that her mother could never fill.**

heal all wounds. She finds herself deftly navigating the often treacherous course called life, using caution with each step lest she detonate another memory. As a means of survival, she has learned to set boundaries. One example is her decision to avoid attending church on Father's Day.

Most other Sundays she's there, mostly because it's what Dad would've wanted. He believed in God. He desired his family to have a firm spiritual foundation. He read Claire Bible stories and prayed with her before kissing her good-night. While Claire wanted to honor her dad's dedication to God and family by making Him a priority in her own life, she had to be honest about it: She was merely going through the motions. Her father's abrupt exit left a cavernous crack in the epicenter of her life that compromised the integrity of her spirit. She knew in her head that she had a Heavenly Father who loved her, but the overriding message from her heart was that you'd better not get too close to Him because fathers can leave you at any moment.

Separated By Disinterest

Patrick had also experienced the agony of abandonment. I first met him at the health club where we were both members. Having similar workout routines, we were often at the club at the same time. Patrick was a fascinating character. His ever-present smile disguised his steely cynicism. Although our conversations at first were surface level—generally fitting into the safe categories of news, weather, and sports—Patrick's contentious attitude made it clear that something threatening lurked beneath the surface.

Patrick managed to keep our conversations shallow until one day he allowed me entrance to a deep place in his soul to which I'm quite sure no one else in his life was granted admission. "My dad called from California. He's got terminal cancer," he said rather matter-of-factly.

"I'm sorry," I said. My mind then immediately went into full-scale counselor mode, as I searched for the right words to help him alleviate his presupposed sadness.

The word search came to an unexpected and abrupt end when he continued, "Don't be sorry. I hope it's a long and painful death."

I had broken one of the rules they teach in counselor school: Never assume another's feelings. A friend of mine learned that when she attended the wake of a former coworker's husband. There is something about visiting a funeral home that prompts even the most well-meaning people to make the stupidest comments, mostly because they think they know how those left behind are feeling. My friend, not wanting to be one of those people, rehearsed in the car what she was going to say. As she stood before the casket arm-in-arm with her widowed friend, she simply said, "Wow. Fifty years. That's a long time to be married to someone."

While exerting great caution not to anticipate her friend's emotions, she was nonetheless taken aback by the widow's response. The woman in black turned to her, shook her head slightly and said, "They were fifty long and miserable years, and I'm glad he's dead."

My reaction to Patrick was the same as my friend's reaction to the merry widow—an open mouth with no words coming out. Correctly deducing that I needed an explanation, Patrick described to me how, when he was just ten years old, his dad decided that being a father was cramping his style. So he bolted. No good-byes. No explanations. No apologies. He just left.

The day he walked out the door was the last time Patrick saw his father. The only tie between him and his family was in the form of monthly child support checks received in the mail. There were never "How are you?" notes included. There were no Christmas cards or birthday wishes. There weren't even any phone calls—until the call to share his diagnosis. If Patrick's father thought the news would evoke sympathy and compassion and would magically undo all the damage he had done to his family,

> **The only tie between him and his family was in the form of monthly child support checks received in the mail.**

he was sadly mistaken. The family tree had been uprooted. In Patrick's eyes, his dad was dead wood.

For the next several weeks, in the whirlpool at the health club and the corner booth at the local hamburger joint, Patrick laid out for me the map of his life's journey since his dad's desertion. Once I knew where he had been it clarified for me how he got to where he was. Understanding his past helped me to piece together the puzzle that was Patrick. His anger now fit—as did his contempt for authority figures. His constant self-deprecation also suddenly made sense, as did his sexual attraction to the man he was living with who, not surprisingly, was old enough to be his father. I now understood his rejection of the mere notion that there existed a god, let alone a Heavenly Father who loved him and wanted a close relationship with him.

The Distress of Abandonment

In America, 24.35 million children (33.5 percent) live absent from their biological father.[10] Whether a father's absence is due to death or desertion, the result is always the same—wounded children who need to be healed. While they may eventually seek healing from boyfriends or girlfriends, pastors or priests, psychics or psychiatrists, support groups or séances, full and lasting recovery from father wounds can only be found in one place: in relationship with the Heavenly Father.

The emotions that Claire and Patrick continue to wrestle with may not be the same. But they share the same fear. It is a fear that has a chokehold on their lives: the fear of abandonment.

Kids whose fathers walk out on their families often suffer greater emotional distress than kids whose fathers die.

Without minimizing the pain a child experiences as the result of a father's death, kids whose fathers walk out on their families often suffer greater emotional distress than kids whose fathers die. Children whose fathers desert the family must live every day with the knowledge that their dads have *chosen* to leave them. It is not an overstatement to say that this thought has the potential to infiltrate every relationship the children will ever have. It is especially poisonous—and sometimes fatal—to their relationship with their Heavenly Father.

A Death with No Body

Another factor that ratchets up the emotional distress level in the lives of children whose fathers have bailed on their families is that it is significantly more difficult for those left behind to achieve closure. There is a finality in death that cannot be realized in the case of desertion. I witnessed this in living color in the life of my friend, Don.

Don was wounded enough when his father, without warning and after thirty years of marriage to his mother, up and went AWOL on his family. But Don's dad did not retreat completely. He stayed within firing range. Months after the divorce, in an effort to appease his guilt, he continued to circle around the family taking pot shots at his ex-wife and kids. The bullets of blame found their mark.

Don tried to fend off the barrage, but his father just kept shooting. Don's dad would call him at all hours of the day or drop in on him at work to complain about how hard his life was, how Don's mother was nothing but a witch with a capital *B*, and how Don never appreciated all that he did for him and the family. Every conversation with his dad sent Don reeling.

His father would then lay low for a while, giving Don the false hope that the battle was over. But just when Don's wounds began to scab over his father would re-emerge and rip them off with fresh accusations.

For a long time Don just kept his mouth shut and suppressed the hurt, trying to convince himself that even a shaming relationship with his father was better than none at all. But one day he had simply had enough. After being interrupted at work for the umpteenth time by a phone call from his father with allegations so familiar he knew them better than the Pledge of Allegiance, he was pushed beyond the threshold of tolerance. In exasperation he countered with a response that is sure to resonate with anyone who has been engaged in a similar manner with an estranged father. When his father paused briefly to reload, Don blurted, "You know something, Dad? Sometimes I wish you were dead. Then I could be done with you."

Don's response to his father provided me with clarity concerning a comment I heard from a woman in a support group I once facilitated. She said, "Divorce is like a death with no body." There is a closure that comes from death that cannot be attained in the case of divorce or desertion. Grieving the loss of a father who died is different from grieving the loss of a father who left by choice, especially when he continually pops up, doing and saying stupid and hurtful things. Whether a father is taken away or walks away, a dad's abandonment needs to be grieved.

> **Whether a father is taken away or walks away, a dad's abandonment needs to be grieved.**

Forms of Abandonment

Death and desertion are not the only ways fathers abandon their children. Many children have been abandoned by fathers who are physically present in the home but who are absent emotionally. Children have been rendered fatherless by dads who use drugs, who drink too much, who work too much, who suffer from mental illness, or who simply have no clue how to be a dad.

These kids aren't included in the 33.5 percent of those living without their biological father. But their reality is the same. All are missing out on the love and affection of a dad.

There haven't been many TV shows that I have watched religiously, but there are two series I have seen every episode of—*The Honeymooners* and *M*A*S*H*. Strangely enough, both have given me valuable insight into fatherhood. *The Honeymooners* made me grateful Ralph Kramden never procreated. If Alice made the veins in his neck pop out as he threatened to send her to the moon, I sincerely doubt a teething child would have survived long in the Kramden household.

M*A*S*H, in one of its more memorable episodes, offered a glimpse into the father-son relationships of two of its main characters. Hawkeye got word in Korea that something had happened to his father stateside, but because of a breakdown in the telephone communication, he had no idea if his father was dead or alive. Hawkeye's friends watched as he desperately pursued every means possible to find out what had happened. His frenetic response spoke volumes about the quality of relationship Hawkeye had with his dad.

In an uncharacteristic moment of empathy, bunkmate Major Charles Emerson Winchester III, even though his father was among the social elite in Boston and provided Charles with anything he could have ever wanted, shared with Hawkeye that he had always been jealous of the close relationship Hawkeye had with his dad. Said Winchester, "Where I have a father, you have a dad." There is a difference.

Effects of Abandonment

Whatever its form, being deprived of a dad's presence in their lives can have devastating effects on children. Common characteristics in children without dads include the following:

- *Low sense of self-worth.* It is very typical for children of father-less homes, no matter what their age, to base their self-worth on the opinions of others. When a father is not involved offering support and encouragement in his kids' lives the interpretation often is, "I must not matter."

- *Feelings of inferiority.* Children can't help but feel lower on the totem pole than friends who have fathers who are actively involved in their lives. They often believe, erroneously, that *all* of their friends have such a connection with their dads. Therefore, no one is lower than them.

- *Taking on blame.* Children cannot process data like adults. A child's logic simply says, "Dad left. It's my fault."

- *Belief that you are unlovable or that something is wrong with you.* This is a part of taking on blame. Children tend to personal-ize abandonment and reason that if only they were better, their fathers wouldn't have left them.

- *Lack of desire to achieve.* A child can soon realize that even be-ing perfect won't bring their dad back so they tell themselves, "why try?" Abandoned boys especially can exhibit a lack of competitiveness and passion.

- *Little self-discipline.* This is commonly referred to as acting out. Children release aggressive impulses to relieve emotional tension.

- *Inability to share feelings.* There are three rules children impose on themselves to help them survive life in a dysfunctional environment—don't talk, don't trust, and don't feel. These rules serve to protect them from feeling pain they would much rather avoid.

- *Either totally rejecting or idealizing the absent parent.* Sometimes children who have been abandoned deal with their pain by completely rejecting the father, who in their eyes has rejected them. They often vow to be exactly the opposite of their father. Conversely, there are situations in which children who have been abandoned receive comfort by creating a fantasy world in which they have a wonderful relationship with their fathers. Known as the "trauma bond," hurting children continually seek acceptance from a parent even though logic tells them it's like putting their hand in a cupboard full of mousetraps. The trauma bond is not based on reality, but on hope or an ideal.

While these characteristics of father deprivation can be quite ravaging in and of themselves, they often lay the groundwork for a lifetime of destructive traits such as pessimism, depression, drug abuse, addiction, cutting, and promiscuity to name a few. It should come as no surprise that the vast percentage of homeless and runaway children, high school dropouts, students exhibiting behavioral disorders, adolescent patients in chemical abuse centers, juveniles in state-operated institutions, and youths in prison grew up in fatherless homes.

The Beginning of Healing

Everyone needs a father's active presence in his or her life. Everyone. Some of us will never experience a close relationship with our earthly fathers. But all of us can experience in our lives the active presence of our Father in Heaven. Believing in and experiencing the presence of a Heavenly Father is the beginning of healing.

Psalm 103 tells us that "The LORD is like a father to his children" (Ps. 103:13, NLT). Granted, to those whose fathers have left them, those words are as uplifting as floaties in a tsunami. But David, the author of that particular psalm, wrote those words in a best case scenario context. The ideal father, David says, is filled with "tenderness and compassion" for his children.

In Psalm 27 David paints a vivid picture of the attributes of our Heavenly Father. Throughout this chapter he acknowledges God as our Light, our Salvation, our Fortress, our Protector, and our Helper. These names remind us that we need never feel afraid when our Heavenly Father is around. But in verse 10 he speaks directly to those who are prone to such fears because of an absent earthly father. He writes, "Even if my father and mother abandon me, the LORD will hold me close" (NLT). It's a personal promise from a Father who has never broken one yet: *No matter what you experience with your earthly father, I will hold you close.*

A Father's Protection

Our son, Greg, was two years old when we bought him his first vehicle. The gift was, in part, to soothe his ruffled feathers for our having the audacity to have a second child. Up until this point, he had been the center of attention. Now he would have to share the spotlight—and with a baby girl, no less. So when we brought Mindy home from the hospital, Greg was duly compensated for his pain and suffering with a shiny, new Big Wheel.

One thing about Big Wheels. Even when they're twenty years old they still have that new Big Wheel smell. Even before we could affix the super cool decals on the frame that would have ensured his popularity among neighborhood two-year-olds, Greg began begging to take his new ride out for a spin. Since he had never before been allowed down the open sidewalk in front of our house, he asked me to accompany him.

He rather enjoyed his newfound freedom. But I couldn't help noticing that he would only travel a few yards at a time before turning around to make sure I was there. My presence provided the safety and security he needed. He would only proceed once he knew his protector was not far behind.

Kids stand a little taller when they know that they have a father who stands behind them.

Sigmund Freud once said, "I cannot think of any need in childhood as strong as the need for a father's protection." Kids stand a little taller when they know that they have a father who stands behind them. Those of us who grew up without experiencing the presence of our earthly fathers in our lives must learn that we too, can stand tall. Our Heavenly Father walks with us.

A "With Us" God

In the very first book of the Bible, our Father in Heaven says, "I am with you and will watch over you wherever you go" (Gen. 28:15, NIV). He then reiterates, "I will not leave you." Also, way back in the Old Testament, our God, when the mantle of leadership was passed from Moses to Joshua, said, "No one will be able to stand against you all the days of your life. As I was with Moses, so I will be with you; I will never leave you nor forsake you" (Josh. 1:5, NIV). For emphasis He then added, "Be strong and courageous! Do not be afraid or discouraged. For the LORD your God is with you wherever you go" (v. 9).

So much does God want to impress upon us the truth that He is always with us that He instructed that Jesus be called *Immanuel*. The name Immanuel is a compilation of two Hebrew words: *Immanu*, meaning "with us," and *El*, meaning "God." Our Heavenly Father is a "with us" God.

Sometimes dads leave. Divorce, death, or disassociation robs kids of their father. But our Father in Heaven is a Father who will never leave. He will never abandon us. God is with us wherever we go. He is behind us to encourage us. He is beside us to befriend us. He is above us to watch over us. He is beneath us to lift us up. He is within us to give us courage. He is before us to show us the way.

In Psalm 139, David brags about our Heavenly Father: "You go before me and follow me. You place your hand of blessing on my head. Such knowledge is too great for me to understand! I can never escape from your Spirit! I can never get away from your presence! If I go up to heaven, you are there; if I go down to the grave, you are there. If I ride the wings of the morning, if I dwell by the farthest oceans, even there your hand will guide me and your strength will support me" (v. 5–10, NLT).

Never Alone

The story is told of the rite of passage from childhood to manhood for boys in the Cherokee Indian tribe. According to legend, for a boy to become a man he must pass this test. The boy's father would take him into the heart of the forest where he was seated on a large stump, blindfolded, and left alone for the night. He was required to stay there with the blindfold on until the rays of the morning sun would shine through it.

He was not to cry out for help. Once he survived the night, he would be considered a man. He was also to vow not to tell the other boys of this experience so that each of them could come into manhood on his own.

The experience was terrifying. Not being able to see magnified every sound the boy heard. His overactive imagination would transform every animal sound and cracking twig into wild beasts and evil humans seeking to do him harm. He was to sit quietly on the stump until morning if he was to become a man.

Finally, after a long, horrific night, the light of the morning sun would filter through. The boy would remove his blindfold. It was then that he would discover that his father was sitting on the stump next to him. His father had been at watch the entire night, protecting his son from harm.

We, too, are never alone. Even when we don't think He's there, our Heavenly Father is watching over us, sitting on the stump beside us. He would never think of leaving His children alone.

His message to us, quilled by the prophet Isaiah: "Don't be afraid, for I am with you. Don't be discouraged, for I am your God. I will strengthen you and help you. I will uphold you with my righteous right hand" (Is. 41:10, NLT).

Write those words on an index card and keep them with you. Memorize them. Personalize them. Meditate on them. Arm your mind and soul with their indomitable truth.

Grasping and Trusting

Some people know very little about their earthly father. Some wish they didn't know what they know. But knowing the truth, the whole truth, and nothing but the truth about our Heavenly Father is crucial to our well-being. So help us God. Healing for our woundedness begins once we search for, firmly grasp, and deeply trust our Heavenly Father's promises to us.

David makes God's truth clear: "Those who know your name trust in you, for you, O LORD, do not abandon those who search for you" (Ps. 9:10, NLT).

Our Heavenly Father will not abandon us. He is a "with us" God. He is always there. When we don't think we're going to make it, He is there. When we don't feel His presence, He is there. When we don't understand why things happen, He is there. When we don't think we will ever experience peace in our life, He is there. When we need Him the most, He is there.

After Jesus was crucified and miraculously rose from the grave, the time had come for Him to leave this earth. His disciples met

Him on a mountain where He was to deliver His farewell message to those closest to Him. Imagine their feelings and thoughts as they climbed that hill: sadness that they would be separated from their friend mingled with curiosity as to what He had to say. For three years He had nurtured them with words of encouragement and instruction, admonition and correction. This was His final opportunity to share what was most important for them to know.

Jesus kept His final address short and sweet. He blessed them. He told them to tell others about Him. Then, just before He was taken up into heaven, he said, "And be sure of this: I am with you always, even to the end of the age" (Matt. 28:20, NLT).

More significant final words were never spoken.

CHAPTER 4

A Father Who Will Always Love Us

*There is more hunger for love and appreciation
in this world than for bread.*

Mother Teresa

Through the years there have been some memorable moments during the Academy Awards presentations:

- Halle Berry becoming the first African-American woman to win the Best Actress Award.

- Marlon Brando sending a Native American woman to accept his Best Actor Award for *The Godfather* who proceeded to chastise Hollywood for its treatment of her people.

- David Niven, as he was about to introduce Elizabeth Taylor to present the Best Picture Award, being surprised by a streaker who ran across the stage.

My favorite Academy Award moment took place back in 1984. Sally Field (who, just to show how old I am, I still remember as *Gidget*) was announced the winner of the Best Actress Award for the movie *Places in the Heart*. As she stood at the podium, clutching her Oscar, she gushed, *You like me! You really, really like me!*

Since I was a little boy, I have been enamored of award shows. I would often dream (okay, I still dream) of having my name announced as the winner of some prestigious award. I picture the audience members jumping to their feet applauding wildly, calling out my name as I ascend the platform, offering congratulatory hugs and handshakes along the way. Once the roar of the crowd dissipates enough for me to be heard, I would humbly accept my trophy, thank several dozen people by name, none of whom are known by anyone else in the room, then, in keeping with Oscar tradition, turn the wrong way when exiting the stage. Sorry. Perhaps that is too much self-disclosure. Yet, if we're honest, don't we all long to receive ovations for our accomplishments? But actually, there is a deeper need. Even more than being loved and appreciated for what we've done, we are born with a deep desire to be loved and appreciated for who we are.

Even more than being loved and appreciated for what we've done, we are born with a deep desire to be loved and appreciated for who we are.

We all need those people in our lives around whom we can be completely comfortable just being ourselves, knowing it won't jeopardize their feelings toward us. We long for relationships with others who know everything about us—every quirk, habit, and idiosyncrasy—and love us anyway. There's something about the marriage relationship that dissolves all pretense. Comedian Gary Shandling contends that the primary reason men get married is so that they don't have to hold in their gas.

If anyone should love us as we are and with no-strings-attached it should be our fathers. The ability and desire to love their children in this manner should be present in the DNA of every father, without exception. The cold, hard reality is it's not. Many children grow up in environments where they don't experience the love of a father as God intended.

The Apple and the Tree

Richard sat on the edge of the examination table which was more a metaphor of his life than he would ever admit. Every time he shifted his weight the one-ply protective paper stretched loosely over the painfully cold plastic made a crinkling sound. He checked his watch for the time. It was exactly sixty seconds later than the last time he checked. Richard shimmied off the table and began pacing as best he could in a doctor's office that was slightly larger and considerably more antiseptic-smelling than the average Porta-Potty.

Richard muttered to himself about "wasting valuable time." He didn't want to be there in the first place. This doctor's visit was only to appease his wife.

The doctor opened the door, greeted Richard with a handshake, and invited him to have a seat. "So what seems to be the problem?" she asked as she cleaned off the handshake with sanitizer.

Richard pulled a piece of paper from his pocket and handed it to her. To save time, he had written out the symptoms he had been experiencing:

abdominal pain
shortness of breath
heart palpitations
muscle tension
lower back pain
diarrhea
butterflies in stomach
inability to concentrate
restlessness
mood swings
inability to sleep

"So what's going on with me?" he asked. "I feel like I'm falling apart. Is there some kind of pill you can prescribe?" he asked.

The doctor forced a smile and secured the list on her clipboard. She looked Richard in the eye, folded her arms across her stethoscope and said, "Tell me about your schedule."

Richard silently wondered if doctors were required to take a course in condescension. "My schedule?" he snorted. "What's that got to do with anything?"

The doctor explained. "Generally, when someone has a host of symptoms like these the problem is stress. So how about you tell me what an average week looks like for you."

Richard wasn't buying what he saw as a hasty diagnosis. But he humored her and shared with the doctor a typical workweek. By the time he got to Tuesday the doctor slumped against the desk, feigning exhaustion from merely listening to his busyness. As he continued, it became obvious that in addition to his out of control work schedule, Richard was also overcommitted at church. He led meetings during the week. He taught classes on weekends. He served as an usher. If the church doors were open, he was there. Clearly, Richard had all of the characteristics of a classic workaholic.

When he finally finished his week-in-review, the doctor, veiling her disdain, surmised the situation. "I can prescribe medication to ease some of your discomfort, but if you want to be rid of your symptoms, you need to change your way of life. You have to stop burning the candle at both ends."

After mulling over her assessment for two Mississippi's, Richard responded, "How about you just write me a prescription for more candles?"

The doctor was not amused.

Fortunately for Richard, this conversation, his intensifying medical issues, and his wife's continued prodding (to use a more church-friendly term) led him to make an appointment with a therapist.

By the time their first session had concluded, even though his male ego demanded he keep his mouth shut, Richard made an admission. He confessed it was time to assess and address his lifestyle.

But first, as his therapist recommended, he had to take a serious look at some underlying factors that were prompting that lifestyle.

Richard personified the adage, *the apple doesn't fall far from the tree.* Seventy-hour work weeks were the norm for Richard's father. His dad wore his workaholism as a badge of honor. He often volunteered to work overtime even though he didn't need the money. To put it nicely, Richard's father was a hard-working, conscientious man who took seriously his role as family provider. To put it honestly, he was committed to his work to the exclusion of the family he liked to think he was "providing for."

When Richard was a child, his father never had time or, more appropriately, never *took* time for his son. Richard can't recall an instance when his dad tucked him in

> **He was committed to his work to the exclusion of the family he liked to think he was "providing for."**

at night. If his father was home from work when Richard was going to bed, he was usually asleep on the couch in front of the television. Richard's dad never took him to a movie, either just the two of them or with the family. He said he didn't want to "waste" two hours when there were things that "needed to be done." Richard's dad skipped every parent-teacher meeting from kindergarten on complaining, "They schedule those things at the worst possible times." Richard would have done cartwheels had his dad even taken the time to ask him about his day.

Richard was starved for his father's love and attention. But he had no way of knowing how to go about getting it. As kids deprived of a father's love often do, Richard viewed himself as the problem. A child's reasoning concludes:

a. Dads are supposed to love their kids.

b. I don't feel loved by my dad.

Therefore,

c. I must be unlovable.

A confrontation Richard had with his father when he was eighteen years old proved this theory in his mind.

Somehow Richard's high school graduation ceremony didn't take precedence over his dad's latest work project. As was his habit, Richard immediately tried to rationalize his father's neglect, cushioning the hurt by telling himself that something really important must have come up. But this offense was too egregious to be overlooked. There was no justifying his dad's decision to blow off seeing him receive his diploma. Richard not only *wanted* his father to be at his graduation, he *needed* him there. Four years of exemplary academic achievement, lettering in three sports, and sitting first chair in the trumpet section were all neutralized by the vacant seat next to his mother.

It took Richard three days to muster up the courage to talk to his dad about it. He secretly hoped his dad would recognize his neglect before it had to be pointed out to him. Richard was disappointed yet again.

When their face to face finally happened, Richard found himself unable to be completely honest about the level of pain his father's delinquency had caused. While beginning to conquer rationalization, Richard was still prone to minimization. So instead of hitting his father full-force with how he really felt Richard watered down his hurt, sadness, and anger by telling his father how "disappointed" he was. Richard was stunned that even his softened approach drew such an immediate and defensive response. "You should be grateful," his dad growled. "Do you think I *want* to work this much? I'm doing it for you. If I didn't work so hard, you wouldn't have all the nice stuff you have."

Richard was defenseless. Blindsided by a wave of shame. Washed away was the simple truth that Richard didn't want nice stuff as much as he wanted a father.

Richard didn't want nice stuff as much as he wanted a father.

Quantity vs. Quality

The significance of a father's love in the lives of his children is immeasurable. The results of a study, published in Personality and Social Psychology Review, suggest that the love of a father is just as important, if not more so, than a mother's love. Researchers concluded that children and adults experience the same level of acceptance or rejection from each parent, but the influence of a father's acceptance or rejection has a greater effect.

Research has found that the love (or lack thereof) of a father affects a child's behavior, self-esteem, emotional stability, and mental health. While this is also true of a mother's love, Ronald P. Rohner, Director of the Center for the Study of Parental Acceptance and Rejection at the University of Connecticut, states that in some cases, "The withdrawal of a father's love seems to play a bigger role in kids' problems with personality and psychological adjustment, delinquency, and substance abuse."

The presence of a father's love in the lives of his children boosts their sense of well-being and actually improves their emotional and physical health.

But clinically proven facts aside, fathers today, often in an effort to justify their schedules, continue to downplay their role in the lives of their children. They excuse their lack of regular involvement in their kids' lives by reasoning that it's not the "quantity" of time they spend with their children that's important, it's the "quality" of that time. There is an old Latin term that describes that disturbingly popular credo: *loadus of crapicus.* Kids need their fathers' love and nothing shows that love more than spending time with them.

After months of therapy, Richard could finally link his own workaholic lifestyle to his desperate desire to gain his father's approval and love. He could also see that the physical

Kids need their fathers' love and nothing shows that love more than spending time with them.

issues he was facing were, in fact, just symptoms of the real problem. Richard suffered the effects of father-love deprivation. Those effects encompassed more than a strenuous schedule and a sensitive stomach. Richard had a scarred spirit.

The Parallel

Richard's counselor pointed out a profound parallel between his relationship with his dad and his relationship with God. Just as Richard was running himself ragged trying to earn his earthly father's love and acceptance, he was doing the same with his Heavenly Father. Richard had become convinced that a father's love was something that must be earned. As a result, his relationship with his Heavenly Father was nothing but a flurry of activities that begged like puppies in a pet store window, "See me. Notice me. Love me."

Those who are father-love deprived are an ever-growing population. At the core of countless souls is found an empty abyss where a father's love should be. Many spend their lives trying to fill that void. But often, when the love we're looking for can't be found, we seek to fill the expanse with cheap substitutes that serve only to magnify the emptiness.

Only a father can satisfy our father hunger. When our earthly fathers leave us wanting, our Father in Heaven stands ready to fill our souls with His love; a love that flows from springs that never will run dry. We are not doomed to a life of emptiness and regret—the inevitable results of looking for love in all the wrong places. If we choose to look in the right places, we can experience, perhaps for the first time in our lives, the warm, inviting, intimate love of a Father. The choice is ours. But making the right choice involves discernment. That's because we have a deceitful enemy who is literally hell-bent on keeping us and the God of love apart.

Satan continually whispers into our ear,

God would never love you.

You don't deserve to be loved.

If God really does exist, He's got more important things to do than spend time with you.

God is just as disappointed in you as your father was.

You will never find the love you're looking for.

Our internal b.s. detector may sound an alarm when we hear these messages. It should. They are lies that smolder because of where they originate. Yet we often subconsciously operate as if they were true. And the enemy wins. Anything he can do to drive a wedge between God and His kids makes the devil cackle with glee.

Look over those lies of Satan again. Do we really think that by adopting them as truth it will help us to experience joy and happiness in our lives? If we ever hope to find healing from father-love deprivation we must do more than say no to Satan's lies. We must say yes to God's truth.

Just Say Yes

You may recall the drug and alcohol abuse prevention campaign that began in the 1980s, *Just Say No*. The initiative began innocently enough. When first lady Nancy Reagan was visiting a school in 1982, undoubtedly wearing a red dress, she was asked by a female student what she should do if someone offered her drugs. Nancy Reagan's response, "Just say no," became *the* strategy for combating drug abuse among youth in America. Sounds easy. Someone offers you drugs, you just say no.

If only it was that simple. The primary flaw of this mission was that the focus was solely on the negative. Kids were warned over and over of the negative consequences of drug use—drugs are addictive, drugs damage brain cells, drugs induce harmful behaviors, drugs can kill you. While these things are true, teens don't need to be told what bad things will happen to them if they make bad decisions as much as they need to hear what good things they could achieve by making good decisions.

There is truth in the statement: You can catch more flies with honey than with vinegar. I wish those of us who have taken on the name Christian would understand this. Many of us are found repulsive to those we are called to love because we reek of vinegar. Christians need a reminder that the word *gospel* means "good news." No matter how you slice it, hearing "If you don't believe as we do you will be thrown into a lake of fire for all eternity" isn't good news.

We all have choices. No matter how difficult life is, no matter what circumstances we find ourselves in, no matter how great our pain, we still have choices. When those of us with father wounds choose to adopt the messages of Satan we are choosing to stay stuck in our misery. It's as if having a bad dad gives us license to carry a chip on our shoulders. We trudge through life feeling sorry for ourselves, lashing out in anger at anyone who crosses us and blaming others for all our woes. And the cycle of dysfunction continues. We treat our kids the way we were treated. We become bad parents ourselves.

Being hurt by our fathers may very well be a *reason* we think and act the way we do. But it is never an *excuse*. We are responsible for our own thoughts and actions. We can choose to let all the negativity stemming from our relationship with our fathers become the legacy we pass on to our children or we can choose to break the cycle of oppression. We can say yes to becoming people of grace, kindness, and forgiveness.

When we recognize what we're saying yes to, it becomes easier to say no to things. If I say no to my wife's idea to have friends over for dinner, it may be because I am saying yes to spending a quiet evening at home with the two of us. If I say no to my wife's Dutch apple pie, it may be because I am saying yes to getting back into my size 34 waist jeans. If I say no to my wife's sexual advances—okay, that will just never happen. But I'm sure you get my point. We can more readily say no to Satan's lies when we have a better understanding of God's truth.

The Bible not only *contains* God's Word, it *is* God's Word. And God's primary word is love. God's great love for His children is interwoven throughout its sixty-six books, almost twelve hundred chapters, and over three-quarters of a million words. The Bible is God's love letter to us.

As is true in the case of our earthly father, we will love our Heavenly Father to the degree that we know Him. So what do we know to be true about the love of God?

> As is true in the case of our earthly father, we will love our Heavenly Father to the degree that we know Him.

His love is sacrificial. We've all seen people holding up *John 3:16* signs at football games. (Just once I'd like to hold up a sign in church that says *Go Bears.*) John 3:16 is the most well-known verse in the Bible: "For God loved the world so much that he gave his one and only Son, so that everyone who believes in him will not perish but have eternal life" (NIV).

Despite the familiarity most people have with these words, the sacrificial love they describe is lost on many folks because it doesn't mesh with their preconceived notions about God's basic demeanor. It amazes me how many people, both in and outside the church, view God as an angry Deity who spends His time grinding axes with anyone who annoys Him. One would think this verse would debunk that bunk.

God so loved that He gave. He allowed His Son, Jesus, to die, effectively paying in full the price of our sins. An angry, vengeful God would never do that. An angry, vengeful God would say, *You got yourself into this mess, you get yourself out.* But ours is not an angry, vengeful God. He is a God of love and He proved that love by making the ultimate sacrifice—the death of His Boy.

As a parent, I cannot imagine a worse pain in life than the pain of giving up a child. When our son Greg was eight years old he walked with his baseball team in our town's Independence Day Parade. My wife and daughters were also in the parade riding on our church's float. Because I was the only one not important enough to be in the parade, I chauffeured my family to the beginning of the parade route, waved at them as they walked by, then drove home when the parade was over. Since the parade route ended a block from our house the plan was for Jan to walk home with the kids.

I was home for some time waiting for my family when suddenly someone began pounding nonstop on our front door. I opened the door to find a frantic, out-of-breath teenage boy who gasped, "Call an ambulance. I hit a kid."

I ran to the kitchen, called 911, and said, "Apparently someone's been hit by a car." I gave our address then went outside to see what had happened.

A large group of people was standing in our street. I made my way to the center of the circle to see if I could help. To this day, when I close my eyes that horrible picture pops up on the screen of my mind. There was *my son*, sprawled out on the pavement, motionless, his eyes fixed and staring into space, blood streaming down his face. I have never felt a pain like that before. I hope to never feel it again.

Before the ambulance came, Greg began blinking. He was soon looking around trying to figure out what all the fuss was about. He tried to get up so he could go home, but was held down by his mother until the EMTs arrived.

After a couple hours in the emergency room, we exhaled in relief and quietly offered a prayer of thanks when hospital tests revealed the extent of Greg's injuries: a fractured skull, a broken clavicle, and a relatively minor head laceration. But for several seconds as my son lay bleeding on the asphalt, I felt what God must have felt when He saw His Son sprawled out on a cross, motionless, eyes fixed, blood streaming down His face. Good Friday will never be the same for me. The overpowering depth of God's love was proven on that day. God loves us so much that He was willing to go through the worst pain imaginable—losing a child—to restore our relationship with Him.

"God showed how much he loved us by sending his one and only Son into the world so that we might have eternal life through him. This is real love—not that we loved God, but that he loved us and sent his Son as a sacrifice to take away our sins" (1 John 4:9–10, NLT).

> **God loves us so much that He was willing to go through the worst pain imaginable—losing a child—to restore our relationship with Him.**

Real love, indeed.

His love for us will never end. The Bible tells us that God is love. He is not just love-*ing*. He is *love*. The Bible also tells us that God never changes. So if (a) God is love, and (b) God never changes, we can be reasonably sure that (c) God is, was, and always will be love. The prophet Isaiah calls Him our Everlasting Father.

In our Father's love letter to us He confirms:

- "For [I am] good. [My] unfailing love continues forever, and [my] faithfulness continues to each generation" (Ps. 100:5, NLT).

- "I have loved you, my people, with an everlasting love. With unfailing love I have drawn you to myself" (Jer. 31:3, NLT).

- "For the mountains may move and the hills disappear, but even then my faithful love for you will remain" (Is. 54:10, NLT).

Our Heavenly Father's love for us bears no expiration date. We can't outlive it. We can't truly live without it.

His love is personal. As I mentioned earlier, the Bible contains dozens of different names for God, each of which gives us a glimpse of His multifaceted nature. There is one name that has consistently drawn me into a closer, more intimate relationship with Him. Although the soundtrack to the chick flick *Momma Mia* almost ruined it for me, I still manage to think warm thoughts when I hear the name *Abba*. Best translated as "Daddy," there is perhaps no stronger term of endearment for God found in Scripture.

In the book of Romans we read: "For all who are led by the Spirit of God are children of God. So you have not received a spirit that makes you fearful slaves. Instead, you received God's Spirit when he adopted you as His own children. Now we call him, 'Abba, Father.' For his Spirit joins with our spirit to affirm that we are God's children" (Rom. 8:14–16, NLT).

I find it interesting that some Christians find it blasphemous or, to use a less churchy word, irreverent to refer to Almighty God as "Daddy." I once conducted a chapel service at a Christian convalescent home where I spoke on the topic of intimacy with God. I concluded my little talk with a prayer in which I addressed God as "Daddy." Before shuffling off to the dining room an elderly couple, with all the tact of a charter member of the World Wrestling Federation, expressed to me their extreme displeasure at my "blatant disrespect" of a holy God by referring to Him in such human terms.

On my drive home I wondered what it would be like to be in relationship with a God of whom we were so fearful that intimacy was not permitted. A relationship with a Heavenly Father that is permeated with fear is often reflective of the lack of physical and emotional closeness children had with their earthly father. Those children are doubly deprived.

If we are fearful to be in the Heavenly Father's presence we can be sure that feeling didn't come from Him. The Bible states that God doesn't give His children a "spirit of fear; but of power, and of love, and of a strong mind" (2 Tim. 1:7, NIV).

Calling our Heavenly Father "Abba" or "Daddy" is scriptural, encouraged by Jesus Himself. Referring to God as "Daddy" suggests warm intimacy, the kind of love our Father in Heaven wants to receive from and give to His children, *especially* those of us who never attained that deeply personal connectedness with our earthly fathers. God is a Daddy who goes to great lengths to affirm His love for His kids.

> **God is a Daddy who goes to great lengths to affirm His love for His kids.**

His love for us never changes. Human love is fickle. Although the rock band Boston tried to convince my generation that love is "More Than a Feeling," human love is all too often based solely on feelings. The danger of feelings being the foundation of our love for someone is that feelings come and go. Basing a relationship on feelings is like trying to build a skyscraper in a swamp.

Even the term "falling in love" suggests instability. Stable, strong, focused people don't fall. The country song "I Fell in a Pile of You and Got Love All over Me" only proves my point.

In his book *The Road Less Traveled*, psychiatrist M. Scott Peck writes, "Love is not a feeling. Love is an action, an activity…Genuine love implies commitment and the exercise of wisdom." We can't "fall into" that kind of love. We "step into" it.

Read carefully these words from the book of James describing our God's love for us: "Whatever is good and perfect comes down to us from God our Father, who created all the lights in the heavens. He never changes or casts a shifting shadow. He chose to give birth to us by giving us his true word. And we, out of all creation, became his prized possession" (James 1:17–18, NLT).

Some of us grew up in homes with shifting shadows. We didn't know from one moment to the next what to expect. Love and stability routinely gave way to turmoil and chaos, often without notice. We found ourselves wanting to walk in love but wound up walking on eggshells. Our father's love could be pulled out from under us at any moment, for any reason.

In the Bible, James makes it clear—our Heavenly Father doesn't love us like that. There are no shifting shadows in His relationship with us. His love for His kids never changes. It cannot be altered by bad moods. There can be no falling out of His love. There's no walking on eggshells around Him. We can, with complete confidence, step into love with the kind of Father who brags that we are *His prized possession.*

Those of us deprived of a father's love often go through life feeling as if we're missing the credit hours needed to achieve a degree of normalcy.

His love is all-encompassing. Those of us deprived of a father's love often go through life feeling as if we're missing the credit hours needed to achieve a degree of normalcy. While it seems everyone around us has graduated to a life of fulfillment and contentment, our report card still has *incomplete* written across it in red letters.

But in our Heavenly Father we have a Teacher who offers to tutor us for as long as it takes to not only complete the course, but to graduate with honors. His passion is that His children experience life to the fullest, that we are made complete. There is just one prerequisite: We must fully grasp the concept of His all-encompassing love.

Check out the lesson plan He has for us: "And may you have the power to understand, as all God's people should, how wide, how long, how high, and how deep his love is. May you experience the love of Christ, though it is too great to understand fully. Then you will be made complete with all the fullness of life and power that comes from God" (Eph. 3:18–19, NLT).

When we *experience*—not just *know about*, not just *feel*, not just become *familiar* with, but when we *experience*—the width, the length, the height, and the depth of His love, *then* we will be *made complete with all the fullness of life and power that comes from God.*

We must experience the width of God's love. It covers every corner, every crevice, every square inch of our life.

We must experience the length of God's love. The love He has for His children will not only last as long as we live on this earth, it will continue on through eternity. Like the Energizer Bunny and, more to the point, the commercials that feature him, God's love for us will keep going and going and going....

We must experience the height of God's love. As David penned in one of his Psalms, God's love is "as high as the heavens are above the earth" (Ps. 103:11, NIV). To borrow a phrase from Buzz Lightyear in the movie *Toy Story*, God's love stretches "to infinity and beyond!"

We must experience the depth of God's love. It doesn't just stretch up to meet us when we're on the mountain as we're reflecting that life couldn't possibly be better, it reaches down to embrace us when we find ourselves in the depths of despair wondering how we can possibly go on.

When I ponder God's all-encompassing love for me, I can envision Him swaying with outstretched arms as He breaks into a little Diana Ross: "Ain't no mountain high enough, ain't no valley low enough, ain't no river wide enough to keep me from gettin' to you." (In my original version I saw Him holding a lighter in the air, but then I realized He probably doesn't smoke.)

We can never be separated from His love. In Romans 8, hands-down one of my favorite passages of Scripture, Paul, after explaining what it means to belong to Jesus and be controlled by the Holy Spirit, offers a brief Q & A session.

Q. "Can anything ever separate us from Christ's love? Does it mean he no longer loves us if we have trouble or calamity, or are persecuted, or hungry, or destitute, or in danger, or threatened with death?" (Rom. 8:35, NLT).

A. "No, despite all these things, overwhelming victory is ours through Christ, who loved us. And I am convinced that nothing can ever separate us from God's love. Neither death nor life, neither angels nor demons, neither our fears for today nor our worries about tomorrow—not even the powers of hell can separate us from God's love. No power in the sky above or in the earth below—indeed, nothing in all creation will ever be able to separate us from the love of God that is revealed in Christ Jesus our Lord" (Rom. 8:37–39).

Allow me to offer my own personal translation.

Q. *Can anything ever separate us from the love of our Heavenly Father?*

A. *No way! Nothing that comes our way, neither abuse nor addiction, neither downsizing nor depression, neither financial setbacks nor family sickness, neither disabilities nor a dad's defection will ever be able to separate us from the love of God that is in Christ Jesus our Lord.*

What God has joined together let not the problems of life separate.

His love is unconditional. Unconditional love is just that— love without condition. Our Heavenly Father's love is not based on what we do. It is not dependent on our conduct. We can't possibly do enough good deeds to earn it. We can't possibly do enough bad deeds to lose it.

The thought of being loved unconditionally is foreign to many of us because our dads didn't speak that language. We were taught that love was given only when certain criteria were met. Conditional love is "if/then" love. *If* you love me, *if* you meet my standards, *if* you live up to my expectations, *then* I will love you.

Conditional love is hardly ever stated, but it is often implied. Fathers who love conditionally withhold it when their children do something wrong or upset them in some way. That is the unfortunate feature of conditional love—it can be turned off at any time.

If how our dads related to us is our primary frame of reference, it becomes clear why so many of us struggle to fully experience the love of God in all its glory.

If how our dads related to us is our primary frame of reference, it becomes clear why so many of us struggle to fully experience the love of God in all its glory. When our earthly fathers attach strings to their love it seems right that our Heavenly Father would do the same thing. Even when we have *heard* that our Heavenly Father's love is unconditional, even if we *want* to believe that what we heard is true, our *experience* is that a father's love is given only when conditions are met.

When we impose our father's faulty, flawed methods onto God we come to believe that God will withhold His love until we meet His standards; that God will love us when we're good but not when we're bad; that God will love us only when we have duly proven ourselves worthy of it. All are lies from the evil one; an anvil he places in our hands as God dangles His love above our heads.

For us to experience the flowing of our Heavenly Father's unconditional love in our lives we must cast off Satan's lies and embrace God's truth. God loves us just the way we are. God doesn't deny His love until we achieve a certain level of righteousness. God won't stop loving us when we make mistakes. There is not one single model of unconditional love that comes equipped with a shutoff valve.

The apostle Paul writes of our Heavenly Father's love: "You see, at just the right time, when we were still powerless, Christ died for the ungodly. Very rarely will anyone die for a righteous man, though for a good man someone might possibly dare to die. But God demonstrates his own love for us in this: While we were still sinners, Christ died for us" (Rom. 5:6–8, NIV). You see, He doesn't love us because *we* are good. He loves us because *He* is good.

Ours is a God who not only *says* He loves us, He *demonstrates* that love. He proves it over and over again. He offers the kind of love our souls ache for.

In his book *Soul Cravings*, Erwin McManus writes:

We all need to be loved. We all need compassion. We all need forgiveness. We all need acceptance. And this is why above all else, we need God. We were created to bask in the unending and unconditional love of God. Every good thing our

soul requires we will find in Him. All that we have not experienced from others we can experience in Him. All that our
souls long for can be satisfied in Christ. While we may never
find or receive the love from others that our hearts are desperate for, we can receive a love even greater than that of which
we were deprived.

That is the truth about the Heavenly Father's love for us. It is
stated and reiterated throughout Scripture because He doesn't want
even one of His kids to miss it.

Several years ago, I met a young woman who confessed to me
that she was a Christian in name only. Although she went to church
religiously, she was missing out on the personal relationship with
God that so many of her friends showed evidence of having. When
she didn't find that personal God by attending mass, one of her
friends suggested she buy a Bible. Her priest advised against it, telling her she would find it too confusing. Besides, he said it was his job
to tell her what God wanted her to know.

Thankfully, she ignored his advice. She not only purchased a
Bible of her own she changed churches. She embarked on a spiritual
adventure that led her to the church where I was pastoring at the
time. It was gratifying to witness up-close and personal her gray-
toned faith bursting into vibrant color as she began to discover, by ex-
ploring God's Word for herself, just how much her Heavenly Father
loved her. I still remember where she was standing in the church
foyer when she hugged her Bible like a prized trophy as she gushed,
"God wrote this for *me*! He loves me! He really, really loves me!"

CHAPTER 5

A Father Who Protects Us

The closer we walk to the Shepherd,
the farther we are from the wolf.

Anonymous

Several years ago I led a worship chapel at a Christian elementary school. I wanted to introduce a new song that morning. Its powerful, yet tender lyrics spoke of God being our Shepherd. I thought I would set it up by asking one of the children to share with the rest of the student body what a shepherd is.

Certainly, I thought, the chosen child would offer words like *protector, guide,* or *provider,* any of which would be a perfect lead-in to the song. So with the accompanist playing softly in the background, I asked, "Who can describe a shepherd?" Several hands went up in the air. I picked an unassuming little kindergarten boy to provide my transition. I knelt in front of him and asked, "Can you describe a shepherd for us?"

The boy pressed the microphone against his lips and bellowed loud enough to not require amplification, "He's a guy with a big steel hook and when the sheep get out of line he yanks them by the neck."

So much for my perfect segue. Perhaps W.C. Fields was right. You should never work with children or animals.

But the candid response from that little boy made me wonder how many people view God not as a tender protector or provider but as a stern enforcer with a big steel hook who yanks us by the neck when we get out of line.

God Our Shepherd

The Bible frequently refers to God as a shepherd. To more fully appreciate the significance of that moniker, we must not only understand the role of a shepherd, but the mannerisms of the animal for which he cares.

Sheep have a well-deserved reputation for not being incredibly bright. You've never heard anyone referred to as being smart as a sheep.

Sheep have been known to walk directly into ponds to get a drink, only to get stuck in the mud and drown. Sheep don't have sense enough to go out looking for food when they're hungry. They have to be led to it. They don't have the instincts that other animals possess in terms of finding their way around. Sheep get lost easier than a Mennonite in Manhattan.

While most other creatures in the mammalian class find their tongues to be particularly useful (try saying that without using your tongue), for sheep having a tongue is about as beneficial as having a uvula. Many mammals lick their young after birth to clean them, as well as to stimulate their breathing and digestion. Mother humming-birds lick rain water off their chicks to warm them. Geckos clean their eyes by licking them (the thought of that makes me shiver—I need to be sedated for a glaucoma test). Cats, since they don't sweat like humans, lick themselves to cool off. Our dog, Gizmo, licks him-self because he simply enjoys offending our dinner guests. But while all sheep have tongues, they use them solely to add more vibrato to their baas. Sheep don't lick themselves or their young for any reason. That explains the smell.

Sheep's eyes are only slightly more valuable to them than their tongues. Sheep don't possess keen vision which is why they're so skittish, especially in the dark. Sheep are also known to lack the agility that most four-legged animals have. If a sheep falls on his back he cannot get up by himself.

Can you see why it takes a special person to be a shepherd? Sheep are exceedingly needy animals. A good shepherd makes sure all those needs are met.

The primary responsibility of a shepherd is to provide nourishment for the sheep. Sheep are totally dependent upon the shepherd for food and water. If there are no sources of drinking water in the vicinity, shepherds will either dig a well or collect water from melting snow in buckets to give to the sheep.

Sheep are exceedingly needy animals. A good shepherd makes sure all those needs are met.

Shepherds also serve as protectors of their sheep. They carry rods to ward off wild animals. At night, shepherds in biblical times were known to sleep in the opening of the pen to protect the flock from intruders.

Sheep are familiar with their shepherd's voice. While sheep naturally scatter when alarmed, hearing the voice of the shepherd restores calm.

Another task of a shepherd is to assist mother sheep while they give birth. On the plus side, shepherds don't first have to attend Lamaze classes. Once newborn lambs are delivered, shepherds bring them to the fold. Until the little ones learn to walk, a shepherd will often carry the lambs in his arms or in the fold of his coat.

Most shepherds in biblical days were either the owners of the sheep or close relatives of the owners. Unlike a hired hand, the owner or his family had a vested interest in the sheep. Their ownership of the flock meant each animal was highly valued.

Given these fun facts to know and tell about sheep and shepherds, how might it change your assimilation of the following verses found in the Bible?

- "The LORD is my shepherd" (Ps. 23:1, NIV).

- "We are his people, the sheep of his pasture" (Ps. 100:3, NIV).

- "I am the good shepherd; I know my own sheep, and they know me" (John 10:14, NLT).

- "He will feed His flock like a shepherd. He will carry the lambs in His arms, holding them close to His heart. He will gently lead the mother sheep with their young" (Is. 40:11, NLT).

- "All of us, like sheep, have strayed away. We have left God's paths to follow our own" (Is. 53:6, NLT).

- "For this is what the Sovereign LORD says: I myself will search and find my sheep. I will be like a shepherd looking for his scattered flock. I will find my sheep and rescue them from all the places where they were scattered on that dark and cloudy day" (Ezek. 34:11–12, NLT).

- "I am the good shepherd. The good shepherd sacrifices his life for the sheep" (John 10:11, NLT).

- "For the Lamb on the throne will be their Shepherd. He will lead them to springs of life-giving water. And God will wipe every tear from their eyes" (Rev. 7:17, NLT).

Do you get the picture? In God, we have a Heavenly Father who guides us when we lose our way. He provides for us when we can't provide for ourselves. He understands our needs and tenderly supplies them. He wards off all that would threaten to harm us. He is always on the job; He takes no days off. He is our Protector.

God Our Strength

If I was looking to hire a full-time protector, seeing the words *gentle, tender,* or *nurturing* on a resume would not win the applicant any points. The first adjective I'd be looking for is *strong.* I need my protector to personify brute strength.

Fears and insecurities would melt away if we had an enormous, ever-present enforcer who had our back. God is just that. Point of fact, there's no one bigger or stronger. God makes Marvel's Avengers look like the Vienna Boys Choir. His power and might cannot be matched. So if it's true that He's all-powerful and always on the job, why is it that many of us are still so fearful and insecure?

Author Francis Chan writes, "We serve an all-powerful, amazing, strong God. But we don't focus enough on that aspect of him. Consequently, our churches are filled with people who are scared and weak. It doesn't look right for such a powerful God to have such weak children. Powerful is not an adjective I would use to describe most of the people filling churches today. We should talk about the strength of God. God is strong."[11]

There are many different biblical metaphors that refer to the strength of our Heavenly Father in terms of His protection for His children:

- "God is our **refuge** and **strength**, a very present help in trouble" (Ps. 46:1, KJV).

- "But you, O Lord, are a **shield** around me; you are my glory, the one who holds my head high" (Ps. 3:3, NLT).

- "Trust in the LORD always, for the LORD GOD is the eternal **Rock**" (Is. 26:4, NLT).

- "The LORD is my **rock**, my **fortress**, and my savior; my God is my **rock**, in whom I find protection" (2 Sam. 22:2–3, NLT).

- "The Lord is my **strength** and **shield**. I trust him with all my heart. He helps me, and my heart is filled with joy. I burst out in songs of thanksgiving" (Ps. 28:7, NLT).

From his bio found in the Bible, we know that David, the shepherd boy turned king, was not exactly the bodybuilder type. Yet, when we read his words recorded in Psalm 27, we can picture him puffing out his chest when he brags of God's strength, boasting, "So why should I be afraid? The LORD is my fortress, protecting me from danger, so why should I tremble?" (v. 1–2, NLT)

When we are completely confident in our Heavenly Father's strength we need no longer live in fear. We can strut a little when we know we have a Protector who has not lost to a single foe. If the Undefeated One is for us, who or what could possibly stand against us?

> **We can strut a little when we know we have a Protector who has not lost to a single foe.**

That assurance is especially empowering to those still shuddering from being made vulnerable by an earthly father who was either weak or absent without leave. Confidence comes from knowing that we have a Heavenly Father who is not just present in our lives, He is *very* present. He is our refuge, an impenetrable fortress where no harm can befall us. He is our shield, protecting our honor by deflecting all that would bring us down. He is our rock, an unshakable source of strength and stability on whom we can stand in a world that is fallen. More than offering us strength, He *is* our strength; a strength that is made perfect in our weakness (see 2 Cor. 12:9).

Some of us who read these descriptions of God's power can't help but shout "Amen!" We may have witnessed on many occasions God's protection in our lives and in the lives of people we know. Others are more apprehensive. We *want* to believe we have a Father who will protect us. We *hope* that it's true. We simply need more evidence before we can truly feel secure. Still others don't buy it at all. Not for one second.

Jenna's Dilemma

Jenna had been involved in a Christian women's support group for years. Although attending these weekly meetings helped her make a great deal of progress in terms of dealing with her anxiety, compulsivity, and fear of intimacy, the core problem remained untouched. Stirring in the recesses of Jenna's soul was rage so intense, so combustible, that she was terrified of what she might be capable of if it ever escaped. The lone guard restraining her fury was the shame of her secret.

Jenna had reason to be angry. While there wasn't a lot about her childhood that she could recall, much of what she did remember she had spent her adult years trying to forget. The recurrent dreams that ended in screams made forgetting impossible.

The memories were nauseatingly vivid. She was just a child. He was an adult. He would wait until he thought she was asleep. He would then sneak into her room, pull back the blankets, and while whispering things that were still locked in the safe deposit box in her mind he did things that never should be done to a little girl—especially by her own father.

The sexual abuse increased in frequency and intensity over the years. It continued until the night her mom walked in on them. Jenna was thirteen at the time. Once the restraining order was filed Jenna naively believed that abominable chapter of her life was closed. Though she never saw her dad again, the saga was far from over. A seemingly endless series of emotional and physical maladies, as well as the increasingly labored relationship she had with her husband, had kept her painful story very much alive.

There were times when the ladies in her support group broached the subject of sexual abuse in reference to women they knew or heard about. It was as if Jenna was trapped in a stalled oil tanker in the middle of a wildfire. She endured the random stories, managing to keep a tight seal on her anger, until one day, when an ostensibly innocuous comment sparked an explosion this group of ladies will not soon forget.

One of the women shared concern for her son who was making rather poor choices in terms of relationships and recreational activities. Those in the circle who could empathize rallied around her, offering words of assurance, some of them directly from the pages of Scripture. Jenna felt the surge coming. Then the well-meaning person seated next to the woman with the wayward son put her hand on the woman's shoulder and said, "Just remember: God is watching over him."

For Jenna, that seemingly harmless but slightly righteous remark was the catalyst to years of suppressed rage. Jenna erupted, "So why the hell didn't He watch over me?"

The ladies sat in stunned silence. Jenna held her head in her trembling hands as if she was holding it on. With reddened face and tears gushing the diatribe continued. "I prayed. I begged. I pleaded. He's hurting me. God, make him stop. Make him stop. And what did my 'protector' do? Nothing! So where were you, God? Where were you?"

She needed a Heavenly Father to protect her, not turn the other way.

Jenna needed a father to protect her from harm, not inflict it. She needed a dad to calm her fears, not cause them. Jenna needed a father to wipe away her tears, not give her reason to cry. But most of all, she needed a Heavenly Father to protect her, not turn the other way. The flashbacks of her father's sexual violations continued to haunt Jenna in her adult life. But they were not nearly as disturbing to her as the thought that God stood by and did nothing.

The day Jenna finally unleashed her anger was the day she began to find healing. Until she was honest about what was going on inside she was destined to continue living a life of turmoil. With her secret revealed and her anger acknowledged, Jenna took her first step down the road of recovery. But it was clearing up the misunderstandings she had of her Heavenly Father that led her to discover something that she had never experienced in her life to that point—peace in her soul.

God Our Protector

Jenna's question is sadly familiar: *Where is God when bad things happen in our lives?* The answer we come up with will determine whether we will find the strength and security we seek or be sentenced to a life of weakness and insecurity. Along with Jenna, we need to grab hold of some basic truths about our Heavenly Father.

First, we must understand that even though He is our Protector, God never promises to shield His kids from every problem. Here's a newsflash: Sometimes life is hard and unfair. And it's always been that way. Storylines punctuated by imprisonment, debilitating illness, depression, drunkenness, infertility, adultery, and fatherlessness are not reserved for TV soap operas. Humankind has been plagued by such heartaches ever since sin entered the world. The most beloved biblical characters had skeletons such as these in their prayer closets.

God does not always shield us from evil. But our Heavenly Father *always* protects our identity as children made in His image. Our Heavenly Father *always* provides avenues for us to appropriate our true value and worth. Our Heavenly Father *always* protects us with His ever-present strength in every situation. He may not exercise that strength in preventing bad things from happening to us, but He offers it in abundance to help us from being defined by those things.

> **God does not always shield us from evil. But our Heavenly Father *always* protects our identity as children made in His image.**

There is nothing like hardship in our lives to prove how dependent we are on God. Our relationship with Him deepens during our deepest struggles. It is in times of great adversity that we best understand the greatness of God. When our hearts hurt the most, they connect with His heart the best.

Safety is not found in the absence of danger; it is found in the presence of God. Until we find safety in Him, we will not find it in our other relationships.

Our Heavenly Father is by our side and at this very moment is offering to give us the security, the strength, the power, and the peace that we often cry out for. He specializes in turning heartache into hope, fright into fearlessness, insecurity into invincibility. Only He can bring about these changes in our lives. Maybe, like the shepherd boy David, we just need to ask Him.

Reading David's psalms are like perusing his diary. They allow us to eavesdrop on some of his most personal requests of God:

- "Turn your ear to listen to me; rescue me quickly. Be my rock of protection, a fortress where I will be safe. You are my rock and my fortress. For the honor of your name, lead me out of this danger" (Ps. 31:2–3, NLT).

- "Be my rock of safety where I can always hide. Give the order to save me, for you are my rock and my fortress" (Ps. 71:3, NLT).

- "From the ends of the earth, I cry to you for help when my heart is overwhelmed. Lead me to the towering rock of safety, for you are my safe refuge, a fortress where my enemies cannot reach me" (Ps. 61:2–3, NLT).

David often found himself in potentially abusive, life-threatening situations. He found God in those times as well. In each instance, he was reminded that though his problems were immense, his Protector was invincible.

When Life Stinks

Being an avid gardener, I understand that one of the best things you can do for a flower or vegetable garden is to apply manure from time to time. Not even pricey, factory-processed fertilizers benefit a garden like good, old-fashioned horse doo-doo.

Manure conditions and helps loosen soil, allowing it to retain moisture. It provides plants with much needed nitrogen, keeping them healthy and green. When I dump a little manure on them every so often, I ensure that my flowers will operate at maximum health and intensity. Inside every flower seed, bulb, or root is contained a plant that has the potential to blossom into something truly extraordinary. Manure helps flowers to be all that they were created to be.

The same can be said of us. Even though we get dumped on from time to time with situations that just plain stink, it is in those stinky, smelly times that we can blossom, becoming all that we were created to be.

Unfortunately, many of us can't get past the smell. All we know is that life stinks. We must realize that we have a choice in the matter. We can choose to let our problems define us or refine us. We can make the decision to be victims or be victorious. We can allow the heartaches of life to produce sadness and resentment or strength and resilience.

> **We can choose to let our problems define us or refine us.**

The crappiest times of our lives are the very instances when our Master Gardener can do His best work. I wish I could say that it is in the times when my life is going great that I grow the most, but that would not be truthful. The greatest growth my life happens when circumstances stink the most. There is no more potent human growth hormone in life than pain.

It is said that once when he was briefing reporters President Harry S. Truman referred to a rival politician's address as "a bunch of horse manure." When one of the reporters later expressed to Bess Truman that it was very unbecoming of the President to use such language, she responded, "You don't know how long it took me to get him to say 'manure.'"

So, to preserve this book's G-rating, let's just say God gives us "manure" in life to bring out the very best in us. It causes the greatest growth. It makes us better husbands and wives, fathers and mothers, neighbors and friends, employers and employees. It is in the times of our deepest pain that we have our deepest connection to our Heavenly Father. As only God can do, He wonderfully redeems our most painful, difficult experiences and gives them back to us as gifts that bring us closer to Him.

God Our Hiding Place

There is another fitting metaphor for God found in Scripture that embodies His protective nature toward His children. He is called our hiding place. In Psalm 32 David writes, "You are a hiding place for me; you preserve me from trouble" (v.7, English Standard Version [ESV]).

Our Heavenly Father is a safe place where we can run when we are afraid or lonely. He is a hiding place where we find protection as He holds us close and whispers in our ear that everything is going to be alright. We are safe in Him.

Several months after Hurricane Katrina hit New Orleans, I was part of a volunteer group from our church that went down to Louisiana for a week to help with the ongoing cleanup. While I was saddened by the lingering devastation there was one sight in particular that brought tears to my eyes: seemingly endless mounds of moldy, personal belongings that had been hauled out of people's homes and piled onto the curb.

As I was adding to the pile in front of one woman's residence, I spotted in the midst of relevant rubble a prayer book that had been unceremoniously dumped with the debris by an earlier crew. I opened it to find something that, despite the ninety-five-degree heat with humidity to match, gave me chills. There on the inside cover the homeowner had handwritten these eerily appropriate words from Isaiah 43: "Do not be afraid, for I have ransomed you. I have called you by name; you are mine. When you go through deep waters, I will be with you. When you go through rivers of difficulty, you will not drown. When you walk through the fire of oppression, you will not be burned up; the flames will not consume you. For I am the LORD, your God, the Holy One of Israel, your Savior" (v. 1–3, NLT).

There was no guarantee from God to the homeowner that floods would never come. Just some much needed reminders from our Heavenly Father: *I know your name. I paid a high price for you. You are mine. I will be with you. I am your Savior.* That woman's home was nearly destroyed by Katrina, but her hiding place was untouched. She still belonged to a Heavenly Father who knew everything she was going through and who loved her just the same.

God Our Refuge

The Bible also illustrates God's protection of His children by painting a picture of a mother hen. In Psalm 91 we read, "He will cover you with his feathers, and under his wings you will find refuge" (v. 4, NIV).

I read recently of an interesting discovery in the wake of another natural disaster, a forest fire in Yellowstone National Park. While in the glades assessing the damage of the blaze, a forest ranger happened upon a bird that had perished in the fire but was still standing beneath a tree. The ranger was heartsick with the morbid discovery. He took a stick and knocked the bird over. When he did, three tiny chicks hopped out from under their mother's wings. The mother's instincts had led her to guide the chicks to the ground as the lethal smoke rose upward. Rather than flying to safety, the mother bird chose to sacrifice her life so that her babies could live.

Sometimes dads abandon their kids. Some earthly fathers are not present, physically or emotionally, to provide protection for their children. But our Heavenly Father is present. He provides for His children the security of knowing that He is always aware of our surroundings. And He offers us refuge under His loving wings. Even when floods and fires come—and they will come—we have a Father who is so committed to our safety that He secured it with the blood of His Son, Jesus. God, our Protector, our Refuge, our Shield, our Rock, our Strength, our Hiding Place, our Shepherd offers us what no other father can: *eternal security.*

"The LORD says, 'I will rescue those who love me. I will protect those who trust in my name. When they call on me, I will answer; I will be with them in trouble. I will rescue and honor them. I will reward them with a long life and give them my salvation'" (Psalm 91:14–16, NLT).

> **"When they call on me, I will answer; I will be with them in trouble."**

The truth is God *does* carry a big, steel hook. But it is not a tool of punishment. It is an instrument of care. In stark contrast to being yanked by the neck to keep us in line, God our Shepherd uses that big steel hook to protect us with His love. In what is the most well-known of the 150 psalms, Psalm 23, David says that the rod and staff of the Lord, our Shepherd, "comfort" us.

Every night at sunset, it is common for shepherds to hold out their staff and have the flock pass under it so they can be counted and examined. Having the sheep go through this ritual allows the shepherd to familiarize himself with each animal while observing if any member of the flock is injured or sick.

In the midst of the most distressing father-child relationships we are assured that we have a Heavenly Father who knows us, who loves us, who protects us. May these words of Jesus Himself soothe our spirits: "My sheep listen to my voice; I know them, and they follow me. I give them eternal life, and they will never perish. No one can snatch them away from me, for my Father has given them to me, and He is more powerful than anyone else. No one can snatch them from the Father's hand" (John 10:27–29, NLT).

CHAPTER 6

A Father Who Wants Us To Prosper

The most important job in the universe is to raise a child to love God, to live positively, and to serve humanity.

Dr. James Dobson

A few years back my family traveled to Colorado for a little camping excursion. Even though it was just shy of a thousand-mile journey, I didn't need to utilize MapQuest for this trip. From our home in Indiana, I simply headed west on I-80 until I hit mountains.

To relieve the children's boredom from traveling across Nebraska, which, despite what the map may indicate, is the widest state in the country, Jan initiated an engaging game of I Spy.

Our daughters spied a number of things with their little eyes, all of which were fairly easily identifiable. To prolong the game as much as possible, and to divert our attention from miles and miles of boring blandness, I knew that when it was my turn I needed to spy something that their little eyes couldn't immediately see.

I announced, "I spy with my little eye something that is orange." The most obvious possibilities were traffic cones and snow fences, either of which would have livened up the landscape considerably but neither of which were present in that particular stretch of stratum.

After about sixty seconds of scanning the languid landscape and coming up empty, one of my daughters asked a clarifying question. "Is it inside the car or outside?"

"Outside," I responded, confident that the clue would be of no consequence.

Jan looked at me over the top of her glasses and shook her head (a common occurrence in our thirty-plus years of marriage) and suggested that I might not have been truthful about my sighting. "You see something orange outside?" Her knack of turning a statement into a question would have made Perry Mason plea for private lessons.

"Yes," I said.

"And you still see it?" she asked incredulously.

"Very clearly," I answered. "I'm shocked none of you can."

Our daughters, obviously more trusting of their father than their mother was, begged for hints. *Is it far away? Is it big? Is it on the ground?*

The interrogation went on for the span of seven Cracker Barrels (roughly five miles). They were truly stumped. Finally, convinced that I had milked this game to the very last drop, I revealed my finding. I pointed at a smear on the windshield and said, "Look. Orange bug guts."

It was at this point that Jan imposed a lifetime ban on my participation in family car games.

The moral of the story is this: There is a difference between looking *at* something and looking *through* it. It's true of car windshields. It's true of God's Word.

Missing It

The Pharisees were a colorful, but mostly black and white, group of people. They looked *at* the Bible. They were familiar with every square inch of it. They not only knew every jot and tittle they knew what a tittle was. They committed much of the Bible to memory.

They were self-proclaimed experts on its teachings. Pharisees painstakingly followed biblical rules and insisted others met the same standard.

The gospels never make reference to Jesus rolling His eyes. But if He ever did, you could be sure Pharisees were somehow involved. He had to point out to them on several occasions that, as well-learned as they were, they were missing something. By looking *at* it instead of *through* it, they had missed the *spirit* of the Bible. They were so focused on form they missed out on substance. They were so obsessed with the Bible's religious practices they overlooked its relationship principles. They beat people over the head with the Bible, yet its blatant message of God's love and grace went over theirs. Jesus couldn't have made it any clearer: The greatest commandment of all is to love.

Surely it must break God's heart that many who claim to follow His teachings have missed the most important one. It must grieve Him when His children view Christianity as a rules-based religion when He meant for it to be a relationship based on love. God must weep when people equate His Word with regulation when He intended it to be about transformation.

> **Surely it must break God's heart that many who claim to follow His teachings have missed the most important one.**

Both those who view Christianity as a religion and those who understand that it is a relationship have a basic question they spend their lives trying to answer, but it's not the same question. The religious folk ask, "What does God want *from* me?" Those who live in relationship with Him ask, "What does God want *for* me?"

A Plan to Prosper

So what *does* our Heavenly Father want for His children? What *are* His desires for His kids? It is in looking *through* His Word that we find the answer: He wants us to be in a personal, intimate, trusting, loving, growing relationship with Him as together we navigate the often turbulent waters of life. He wants us to know that whatever comes our way His plans for us will never include fear and discouragement, but will always embody hope and peace.

God's words of affirmation given through the prophet Jeremiah hundreds of years ago to Jewish exiles hold true for His children yet today: "'For I know the plans I have for you,' declares the LORD. 'Plans to prosper you and not to harm you, plans to give you hope and a future'" (Jer. 29:11, NIV).

The kind of prosperity our Heavenly Father has in mind for us is not reimbursement for being righteous, for memorizing and adhering to a religious code of conduct. The Christian faith is not merely about knowing. It's about growing. God's plan for you and me is to make us prosper by helping us to grow in relationship with Him.

Never Good Enough

Try as he might, Lee has a hard time grasping that truth. His spiritual life has come to a screeching halt because he has come to believe two things:

1. God's plans to make him prosper hinge on him being good enough, and
2. He will never be good enough.

During middle school, Lee's band director awarded him with a solo in one of the pieces they were preparing for their upcoming spring concert. For anyone else in the trombone section, it would have been just a four-measure solo. For Lee it was an opportunity to finally measure up to his dad's expectations.

Lee had wanted to play the clarinet when he first joined the band. But his dad told him that woodwind instruments were for girls. Boys belonged in the brass section.

Truth be known, Lee didn't even want to be in the band. But he had an insatiable desire to be in his dad's good graces, and music was a better vehicle than sports. Lee clearly had no athletic ability. He was a clumsy boy—something his dad was quick to point out, often emphasized by an openhanded smack to the back of the head.

Lee wasn't exactly musically inclined either. He had to put a lot more effort into his playing than most of the other students in the band. But he reasoned it would be worth it if it would result in an "attaboy" from his dad.

Lee remembers in vivid and unsettling detail running all the way home one day after school to show off a report card with all A's and one A-minus. His mom gave him an obligatory hug and an "I'm proud of you," which Lee shrugged off as expected. He needed affirmation from his father.

His dad's response? "How does anyone with a brain in their head get an A-minus in English?"

Lee vowed never to get less than an A again. When his next report card reflected all A's he was sure he would get the approval from his father that he craved, or, at the very least, a reprieve from being beaten with the buckle end of a belt. Lee waited until after dinner and before his dad turned on ESPN so he could have his undivided attention. He proudly handed his father the report card.

His dad opened his mouth as if to say something but then stopped himself. The butterflies in Lee's stomach scattered, giving way to a knot that grew tighter with every second of silence. *What would he possibly find wrong with me now?*

"I see you got a tardy," Lee's dad said with a look of disdain. "What the hell is up with that?"

Lee could feel the numbing effects of a toxic mixture of disappointment and fear wash over his body. Now *he* stood with his mouth open and nothing coming out.

His father's words were laced with sarcasm. "You do own an alarm clock, don't you? How can you not get to school on time? Apparently, it's time you learn about responsibility."

With that, Lee's dad pulled off his belt and administered a lesson to his son about how to behave in a responsible manner. It was a far cry from the teaching style his dad used on Sundays when he led his adult Bible class.

Much of Lee's life was spent trying to jump through hoops, only to have his father raise them higher. He hoped with everything in him that the trombone solo would be the final hurdle to gaining his dad's approval.

Much of Lee's life was spent trying to jump through hoops, only to have his father raise them higher.

For weeks (which seemed like years to his next-door neighbors and their dogs), Lee practiced in his bedroom. Over and over again he played those four measures, first honing in on the notes, then detailing the dynamics. A positive yet unintended result of all this repetition was the development of a striking vibrato, a rare sound from a preteen instrumentalist.

On the night of the concert, the moment Lee came out from behind the heavy, forest green felt curtain and walked onto the hardwood stage floor, he began scanning the audience until he spotted his father. For Lee, this night was not so much a ninety-minute concert by a sixty-piece band before a crowd of 350 as it was a twelve-second audition of a son seeking a positive review from the only person that mattered.

Lee's solo was in the first song the band played. It was flawless. Lee nailed it and he knew it. He found it difficult to play through the rest of the concert—partly because he was so anxious to hear his dad's response, partly because it's hard to play a trombone when you're smiling.

After the concert, Lee, with his trombone still in hand, made his way toward his parents who were standing in a large group of people outside the auditorium. By the time he reached them he had received a number of compliments and pats on the back. His mom offered the expected, "great job," as did several others in the group.

Lee's dad was smiling—a good sign. He then stepped forward, put his hand on Lee's shoulder and said loud enough for everyone in the group to hear, "When are you ever going to learn how to play that thing right? You keep pointing the slide to the floor. You've got to sit up straight and hold it higher."

Those words served to seal the six words that had been branded on his soul: *You will never be good enough.* His father never actually verbalized those words. Yet that belief was burned into Lee's being. Well into his adult life that menacing message charred him relationally, emotionally, spiritually, sexually, even vocationally.

Dads Who Exasperate

Many psychologists today teach that it takes seven to ten affirmations to offset the emotional damage caused by one criticism. In many homes, affirmations are handed out about as often as $200 allowances. Parents don't always value the importance of positive reinforcement in the lives of their children. Kids need to continually be built up. They need praise. They need to be in loving, nurturing environments that encourage them to thrive and allow them to fail.

A child's personality is very fragile. Dads who are demanding and demeaning, critical and caustic, rigid and rules-obsessed produce kids who are easily shattered by unreasonable expectations, paralyzed by doubt, and depleted of self-confidence. Fathers have the power to kill a child's spirit.

Psychologist and author Dr. James Dobson says it is a father's

| **Fathers have the power to kill a child's spirit.**

responsibility to shape and guide a child's will, without breaking his or her spirit, his or her sense of value, and his or her self-worth.

It is possible that a dad can cause his children irreparable damage without doing anything that was deliberately hurtful. He may never have abused them physically. He may never have screamed at them in anger or intentionally shamed them. He may simply have neglected to carry out his primary role as a parent—to love, to nurture, to train, to instruct. Even in the absence of blatant abuse, by not fulfilling these core responsibilities a father can impair his children by conveying to them that they are just not worth his time or effort.

Church-going, rules-oriented, encouragement-impaired fathers like Lee's love to quote Colossians 3:20—"Children obey your parents in everything, for this pleases the Lord." They tend, however, to gloss over the very next verse that says, "Fathers, do not embitter your children or they will become discouraged" (NIV).

The words of Ephesians 6:4 also manage to escape these fathers. In that verse the apostle Paul offers a very clear and succinct message to dads: "Fathers, do not exasperate your children; instead, bring them up in the training and instruction of the Lord" (NIV).

God makes it very clear: good parenting skills never include provoking, angering, or exasperating.

That text begins with a warning. Fathers are told what *not* to do—do *not* exasperate your children. Other translations caution dads: "Do not provoke your children to anger by the way you treat them" (NLT), or, "Don't exasperate your children by coming down hard on them" (*The Message* [MSG]). God makes it very clear: Good parenting skills never include provoking, angering, or exasperating. These techniques do not build up a child; they only tear him or her down.

A Father's Responsibility

Paul follows up his warning of what fathers should not do with their children with a challenge of what they *are* to do: They are to "bring them up in the training and instruction of the Lord." To use the down-to-earth words of Eugene Peterson as found in *The Message*, dads must "Take [children] by the hand and lead them in the way of the Master."

It is a father's responsibility to teach his children about their Heavenly Father—not just by giving words of instruction but by setting a godly example. Christianity is more easily caught than taught. Fathers best teach their kids what the Bible says about God's love, compassion, and forgiveness by being loving, compassionate, and forgiving.

Dr. Paul Vitz, Professor at the Institute of Psychological Sciences in Arlington, Virginia, has noted in his writings that there is a common thread in the lives of fanatical, in-your-face atheists (including Karl Marx, Voltaire, Friedrich Nietzsche, and Madelyn Murray O'Hare): Most of them were children of bad or dead fathers. He notes that Sigmund Freud once made the connection between young people losing their belief in God and their losing respect for their fathers.

Dads who exasperate, anger, embitter, discourage, or continually come down hard on their children are not instructing them in the ways of God. They are not aiding in the fulfillment of God's plan to offer children prosperity, hope, and a future.

I have seen the anguish in kids who were beaten routinely by their ultrareligious fathers because of some "sinful" thing they did or said. In not one instance did the beating bring the child into closer relationship with

> **A desire to live for God can never be beaten into children, but it can be beaten out of them.**

God. A desire to live for God can never be beaten into children, but it can be beaten out of them.

More Discipline

A fourth grade teacher at a Christian school where I was doing prevention work asked if I would meet one-on-one with one of her students. She was looking for affirmation that her conclusion was correct—that the boy should be evaluated for Attention Deficit Disorder. It took roughly five minutes in a room with him to know that the assessment was accurate.

I thought it strange that the teacher asked if I would then sit in on the meeting with the boy's parents, but I agreed. She said she needed moral support. After meeting the boy's father, I needed it too.

The teacher lovingly and compassionately expressed to the couple her concerns for their son. She shared various situations that had arisen in the classroom involving the boy, all of which supported an ADD diagnosis. Per the teacher's request, I then explained to the parents what ADD is and how, when it is untreated, it can lead to significant social, behavioral, and emotional problems. I told them that I agreed with the teacher that their son needed to be taken to a doctor for an evaluation.

The words had barely left my mouth when the boy's father stood up and put on his coat. He then tapped his forefinger on the table and said dismissively, "My son does not need a doctor. What my son needs is more discipline and I assure you he will get it."

That encounter took place over fifteen years ago. That little boy is now a young man, twenty-four or twenty-five years old. I think of him often. I wonder what "more discipline" looked like, or, more to the point, felt like. I wonder how his father's response still affects him. I wonder if he still carries bitterness, discouragement, and anger. I wonder if he has ever discovered that this is not how his Heavenly Father operates.

Arms Wide Open

We must recognize that our Father in Heaven truly wants to bless His children. He always has our best interests in mind. His plan *really is* to make us prosper and that prosperity is not dependent on our following the rules. His plan will never include criticism and discouragement. God's desire is to make us prosper with words of affirmation and love. However, His plan is contingent on our growing in relationship with Him.

It is common for kids with father issues to continually strive to make things right in their relationship with their dad so they can feel accepted. It is also characteristic for these kids to continually scan the horizon for affirmation, yet never find what they're looking for— at least not from their earthly fathers. There comes a point where we must stop looking for things that our fathers are unwilling or incapable of giving. We must look beyond the relationship we have with our earthly fathers and see that we have a Heavenly Father who stands before us with arms wide open, eager to prosper us in ways our earthly fathers never could or would—with not just love, but intimacy; not just approval, but acceptance. Nothing pleases Him more than to have a close, intimate relationship with His children.

Hope and healing will always remain outside our reach if we can't take our eyes off the fractured relationship we had or have with our fathers. While God cares deeply about any of our relationships that cause us pain, He is much more concerned about our relationship with *Him*. It is in relationship with our Heavenly Father that we find what we need the most.

It is not true that God revokes His plans to make us prosper if we're not good enough. What a relief. Who of us could ever be good enough to gain the acceptance of an infallible, holy God? Thanks be to Him, we don't have to turn in a flawless performance to win our Heavenly Father's love. He already knows we're not perfect and He loves us anyway.

The Father's Invitation

Because our God wants nothing but the best for His kids, it makes Him sad when He sees us weighing ourselves down with unmet needs, unreasonable expectations, and unresolved issues. So He comes alongside us and offers to carry that burden for us. His invitation is given in the book of Matthew: "Come to me, all of you who are weary and carry heavy burdens, and I will give you rest. Take my yoke upon you. Let me teach you, because I am humble and gentle at heart, and you will find rest for your souls. For my yoke is easy to bear, and the burden I give you is light" (Matt. 11:28-30, NLT).

When we are burdened with discouragement from seeking approval from dads who will never give it, God says, *come to me*.

Come to me. When we are burdened with discouragement from seeking approval from dads who will never give it, God says, *come to me.* When we are overwhelmed with doubts that we could ever be loved for who we are, God says, *come to me.* When we are hurt by the careless deeds and comments from those we depend on to hearten and reassure us, God says, *come to me.*

Contrary to the opinion of Bible-thumping preachers and belt-swinging fathers, our actions, no matter how noble or biblical, don't impress God in the least if our primary motivation is guilt. The Christian faith is not based on the words *do for me.* Instead, our God pleads, *come to me.* We are to come into relationship with our Heavenly Father through His Son and our Brother, Jesus Christ. We must place our trust in Him—not in our ability to follow the rules—to find acceptance.

When we *come* to God through Christ, He invites us then to *take* from Him. *Take my yoke upon you.* A yoke is a carved, wooden beam that connects oxen together to pull a heavy load or cart. Yokes make it possible for oxen to handle a burden they could never carry on their own. Yokes allow animals to share their strength so they can work beyond their capacity.

When we take the yoke of Jesus upon us, we are, in essence, taking on His power. The result is synergistic. By joining with Him, we operate beyond our capacity. He keeps pulling along with us until, together, we get the job done. When we take His yoke on us and follow His lead, we find rest from our burdens.

Being yoked with Jesus also assures us that not only *won't* He leave our side, He *can't* leave our side. By definition, once we take on His yoke, He takes on ours.

When we come to Him and take from Him, God, as explained in this text from Matthew, then makes us this offer: *Let me teach you.* Our God wants us to enter into a relationship with Him so that we can learn from the Master Himself valuable life lessons about how to live and how to love. To prosper in the areas of living and loving is to find rest for our souls.

Nowhere in the Bible does our Heavenly Father say, *come to me and I will take your problems away.* Despite what many "health and wealth" preachers are promising, God never

> **Nowhere in the Bible does our Heavenly Father say, *come to me and I will take your problems away.***

vows to bless His children with problem-free lives. His guarantee is quite the opposite. Jesus said it bluntly: "Here on earth you will have many trials and sorrows." That's our promise. You won't see Grandma cross-stitching that verse and hanging it on the living room wall any time soon. But Jesus wasn't finished with His statement. There is a part deux to this text, an addendum that provides a divine disclaimer. Jesus went on to say, "But take heart, because I have overcome the world" (John 16:33, NLT).

No matter what trials or sorrows we face on this earth, we can take heart. We are yoked to One so powerful that He rose victorious over sin and death and hell. Surely He can handle whatever problems we may face.

Happy Endings

There aren't many things that upset my wife more than investing an hour and a half into a movie that doesn't have a happy ending.

When she's been drawn into characters' lives, when she's grown to like them, when she's found herself pulling for them to overcome their inevitable struggles, she wants a positive payoff. She wants a "happily ever after."

Thanks to Jesus, the life story of everyone who believes His promises will have a happy ending.

In his review of *The Passion of the* Christ, former Chicago *Sun-Times* movie critic Roger Ebert referred to the resurrection of Jesus. He was dumbfounded when he was then criticized by a reader for giving away the ending. Spoiler alert: Jesus wins!

By His death on the cross and resurrection from the grave, Jesus has overcome the world. So even on those days when we can barely put one foot in front of the other, when we're weighed down by trials and sorrows, our load is lightened with the knowledge that Jesus has already overcome each of them.

And what's more, our Heavenly Father not only gives us ultimate victory over the bad things of life, but He takes those bad things and reshapes them into good. It's not just a spiritual sound bite: God never wastes a hurt. So much does He have our best interests in mind that He takes even our most ugly, painful, gut-wrenching experiences and transforms them into opportunities to reflect His goodness.

Pain Redeemed

It is said that we minister best out of our deepest pain. I have seen this time and time again in God's church.

For instance, my friend Wendy knows the pain of having a spouse who was unfaithful. She also knows what it feels like to have been ignored by people from the church mostly because they were uncomfortable and didn't know what to say. While she endured months of sleepless nights, uncontrollable crying spells, and the pervasive feeling that no one could ever understand what she was going through,

God lovingly took her feelings of humiliation, rejection, and isolation and redeemed them.

Today, Wendy's incredible spirit of empathy is even stronger than the aching of her heart years ago. Her private, God-orchestrated ministry is to walk alongside and lend support to women whose souls have been pierced by broken vows. Knowing the subsequent pain of being treated like a leper in the church community, she lovingly reaches out to those who others inadvertently avoid.

My friend John is another example of how God turns bad experiences into good. John has no degrees in counseling, nor even informal training in therapeutic technique. However, John has plenty of life experience when it comes to addictive behaviors. As a recovering alcoholic, he has completed a graduate-level course in grandiosity. He has a master's degree in manipulation, a doctorate in deception. Framed on his wall is a sheepskin of shame. And if I were to seek help in overcoming the dreaded disease of alcoholism, there is no psychologist or psychiatrist, no counselor or clergyman I would want by my side more than John.

The Bible says "[God] comforts us in all our troubles so that we can comfort others. When they are troubled, we will be able to give them the same comfort God has given us" (2 Cor. 1:4, NLT).

I can say with certainty that I would never have written this book had I not grown up in an alcoholic home. Likewise, had I not lived with a father who struggled with alcoholism, I would not be as dedicated a dad, as helpful a husband, as caring a counselor, or as passionate a pastor than if my dad never picked up a drink.

Shining Through the Cracks

Author and speaker Patsy Clairmont shares how God often shines the brightest light in those areas of our lives where we have been broken. She writes: "Picture an empty pitcher with a network of cracks down the front. Now imagine that pitcher filled with light and a lid put on the top. Where does the light shine through: the cracks."

My friend and motivational speaker Jolene DeHeer was referencing Clairmont's illustration while speaking at a high school assembly about helping others to overcome adversity. She excitedly gave Clairmont's analogy and then blurted out, "What I'm trying to tell you is, God wants to shine through your crack." Probably not something you want to say to a group of high schoolers.

We have a Father who knows what is best for us. We may question why bad things happen to us. We may not see what good could possibly come of those

> **We have a Father who knows what is best for us.**

things. But we can rest assured that God's plan is to make us prosper. Let those words sink into your soul: *rest assured*. His offer of hope and a future, made to every one of His children, will never be withdrawn. We only need to open our arms and embrace it.

Marred Hands

The boy lived with his grandmother. Both of his parents had died and Grandma was all he had. One night, Grandma's house caught fire. In an effort to save her grandson who was asleep upstairs, the boy's grandmother, instead of fleeing to safety, climbed the stairs that were engulfed in flames. She never got to him. Her body was later found just outside his bedroom door.

The fire was so spectacular that a large crowd gathered on the street. Suddenly, someone in the crowd said, "I hear something. Someone is in there!" Above the sounds of the crackling fire could be heard the muffled sounds of child crying. No one knew what to do, or, more accurately no one was willing to do what needed to be done. The entire front section of the house was in flames.

Out of nowhere, a stranger rushed from the crowd and ran to the back of the house. He spotted an iron pipe that reached the upstairs window from where the cries were coming. Without giving it a second thought, the man took hold of the blazing hot pipe, pulled himself up to the second story, and disappeared into the smoke.

The people watching couldn't believe what they were seeing. A short time later the man reappeared, making his way down the red-hot pipe with the boy's arms wrapped tightly around his neck.

The crowd burst into cheers. The little boy had been saved!

Weeks later, there was a public hearing held at the town hall to determine in whose custody the boy would be placed since he had no other family.

The boy listened as several people who wanted to care for him were allowed to speak. The first man who stood said, "I could do a lot for the boy. I have a large farm. He would enjoy living in the country."

A kindly woman then took the floor. "I could provide for him," she said. "I'm a teacher. I would see to it that he gets a good education."

The richest man in the community then took the opportunity to speak. "I happen to be wealthy," he said. "I could give him everything he ever wanted."

The chairman asked, "Is there anyone else here who would like to say what they could do for the boy?" From the back of the room rose a stranger who had slipped into the meeting unnoticed. As he walked forward, his hands in his pockets, it was obvious he was in pain. As he reached the front of the room he stood directly in front of the boy.

He slowly removed his hands from his pockets. A gasp went up from the crowd. The boy, whose eyes had been focused on the floor until now, looked up. The man's hands were blackened and raw. The boy cried out as he recognized the man who saved his life. With a giant leap, the boy threw his arms around the stranger's neck and wouldn't let go.

The farmer stood and left. The teacher did, too. Then the rich man exited. Everyone left the town hall, leaving the boy with his rescuer who said not a word. Those marred hands spoke more effectively than any words could.

In the person of Jesus, our Heavenly Father, with arms outstretched, stands before those of us whose lives are void of a father's love and acceptance. His marred hands, with wounds still visible from the rusty spikes that were driven through them, invite us to live in relationship with Him. He longs to care for His children and provide for us a loving, encouraging, nurturing environment in which our prosperity is certain.

> **In the person of Jesus, our Heavenly Father, with arms outstretched, stands before those of us whose lives are void of a father's love and acceptance.**

CHAPTER 7

A Father Who Wants To Hold Us

Touch has a memory.

John Keats

To friends and neighbors he appeared to be a kindly man who was always smiling and ready to lend a helping hand to anyone in need. But Kathleen's image of her father was drastically different.

"I was terrified of him," Kathleen shared. Her father's drinking was out of control; his thinking and behavior more and more irrational. His alcohol-fueled anger led to physical violence. Her father's touch always resulted in pain.

Kathleen recalled how her dad would go out at night and come home with unexplained bruises. Neither Kathleen nor her mother would ever ask him what happened lest they wind up with black and blue marks they didn't want to explain.

"The physical abuse began with my mom," Kathleen recalled. "One time he came home late because he had to stop at the bar and mom and I had already eaten supper. He exploded because we didn't wait for him and he pushed over our dinner table. When Mom tried to calm him down he gave her a backhand to the mouth and made her bleed." Kathleen shook her head in disgust. "He fooled a lot of people. We looked like the perfect family when we went to his business socials."

Kathleen tells the story of her mom and dad going out for dinner one Sunday night with some friends. "When they were late coming home I wasn't so worried because Mom was with him. Not like I was most times when I was sure that he got drunk and got into trouble. So many nights I laid awake when he hadn't come home thinking he had to be in one of three places: jail, the hospital, or the morgue. Then I would hear him stumble through the back door and think, 'he lucked out again.'"

"On that night, they got home around eleven. They were fighting. I held my breath as I listened from under the covers. My dad was accusing my mom of coming on to one of the guys at dinner. When she told him not to be ridiculous, he called her a slut and ripped her new dress off of her. I can still hear the buttons bouncing off the tile floor."

A Boundary Crossed

Despite his threats to kill her if she left him, Kathleen's mom, putting her daughter's safety before her own, packed up their belongings and moved out. At the time, she was unaware of the unconscionable level of abuse her daughter had already endured at the hands of her husband.

"Even when I was a very young child, maybe nine or ten, my father seemed to be obsessed with my sexuality," Kathleen recalled. "He kept telling me I needed to stay a virgin and not become a whore like my mother. I didn't even know what a virgin was. It didn't matter. I wasn't one for much longer. I just wanted my dad to love me. What he did to me was not love."

With her boundaries of innocence obliterated, Kathleen became vulnerable to attack—not just in a physical or sexual sense, but also in an emotional and spiritual sense. Nothing made sense anymore.

Once she became a teen, despite having seen firsthand the destructive effects of alcohol and vowing never to drink like her father,

Kathleen made a discovery: Alcohol helped relieve pain. And since her pain was always present, soon so were bottles hidden in her closet.

Despite also bearing the grotesque emotional bruises caused by her father's violation of her physical boundaries, Kathleen, starved for tenderness and affection, began to satiate her appetite for love with sex. Her desire was legitimate. She just chose to satisfy it in illegitimate ways. The drinking served to numb her conscience enough to pursue with reckless abandon her unbridled longing to be loved.

While at college, Kathleen gave herself to numerous sexual partners. It was when she had given herself to numerous sexual partners *one night* that her moral compass was flicked. She knew she was perilously off-course in her journey toward self-worth. She was trying to fill her soul with things that only left her more empty.

In an effort to get on the right track Kathleen decided to give church a try. To protect her identity, she found one several miles from campus. She walked into the sanctuary hoping it would be just that—a sanctuary; a safe place where she would feel protected

She was trying to fill her soul with things that only left her more empty.

and accepted. She walked out an hour later feeling only more guilt and more shame.

Sabotaged

While in her sophomore year at college, Kathleen began dating a guy who was different from all the rest. He remembered her name. He called her the week after they had sex. He expressed an interest in her. After a month of sexual encounters, he even professed his love for her. The voltage packed in his words, "I love you," caused a surge in Kathleen that the act of sex never produced. Never had any male in her life used that verb with her as the object. But the definition of the word "love" was as cloudy for her bed partner as it was for her.

Contrary to what we learn about romantic relationships from watching reality TV, love involves more than the exchange of bodily fluids. God, who not only created but embodies love, is a God of order. There is a natural progression in God's plan for the development of a romantic relationship. When the phases are taken out of order and the sex part is put before the social, emotional, and spiritual stages, the relationship can be sabotaged from the start.

Because they skipped ahead to the climax without properly establishing the storyline, Kathleen and her boyfriend cheated themselves out of the pleasurable payoff God offers to those who follow the book of love in sequence.

Kathleen's boyfriend soon became bored with their one-dimensional relationship, yet he wasn't all that interested in the other dimensions. To "liven things up" he talked Kathleen into engaging in sexual acts that state law, not to mention God's law, would readily classify as deviant. She participated, thinking surely, that would make him happy to have her as his girl. But an unguarded computer screen revealed that there were several women he had as his girl. With dignity being another common casualty of sexual abuse, it took several more incidents of unfaithfulness before Kathleen mustered the courage to walk away.

Today, Kathleen is a new person. In her newfound relationship with God, she has discovered the loving embrace of a Father. She credits her mother's persistent prayers for bringing about her spiritual transformation, this after her mother was, herself, transformed. "We may give up on God but God will never give up on us," her mother was fond of saying. Indeed, the passionate prayers of a mother avail much.

Even though Kathleen has left the dangerous life she was living, she still faces its consequences every day. Kathleen's past continues to demand payment. Dealing with the complications of HIV has proven less challenging than conquering her still present sense of shame. But her Heavenly Father has been gentle with her. She has found healing in His touch.

Starved For Attention

A child's relationship with his or her father needs to be hands-on—provided his hands are pure. Clinical Psychologist Dr. Kenneth N. Condrell shares,

> In my practice, I see girls with low self-esteem and an ache for a man's attention and love. It is not unusual to see a fatherless teenage girl who loathes herself so much that she cuts herself, scratches her skin or burns herself. I see abandoned girls respond indiscriminately to any male who shows them attention. These girls are so starved for male attention that they overreact to any attention from a male, no matter how little, or how destructive it may be. These girls frequently respond by becoming promiscuous, and many of them grow up with bitter, cynical feelings about men. [12]

Dr. Condrell states that it is common for boys whose fathers are disengaged from their lives to think poorly of themselves and to lack self-discipline. He says, "Often these young men don't have any passion; they drift aimlessly and act lazy. There isn't anything they take pride in doing well."

Condrell concludes that chronic depression and pessimism about life are common characteristics of children from homes with absent or abusive fathers, homes where a palpable love between father and child is missing.

Without the consistent, loving touch of a father, a child is more susceptible to experiencing sadness, loneliness, and isolation. Young children who lack a significant amount of positive touch from their fathers are, as they grow older, inclined to be more aggressive and violent than those who were nurtured by a loving dad who routinely hugged, cuddled, and kissed them. The lack of a father's tender touch can also have an adverse effect on a child's sexual development.

Zig Ziglar, in his book *Better than Good*, shares the startling findings of Dr. Ross Campbell, a psychiatrist from Chattanooga, Tennessee. Campbell stated that in all of his years of research and practice he has never known an adult with a sexual dysfunction—either male or female—who had a father who was kind, gentle, loving, thoughtful, affectionate, considerate, and patient in his words an actions. A father's hands can build his child's life or tear it apart.

A father's hands can build his child's life or tear it apart.

Blessing or Curse?

Despite the forty-year age difference, Marie was one of my closest friends. We shared secrets; not only in the sense that we told each other things we kept under wraps for years but that they were the same things. Our dads had the same disease. "He used to get drunk all the time," she said of her father. "He was a mean drunk. My brother and I were afraid of him. Mom was, too."

She continued, "I remember the three of us at the kitchen table eating supper one night when he came home. Right away, he started yelling and cussing at us for anything he could think of. My brother and I were little at the time. We started crying. When Mom defended us, my dad raised his hand to hit her. My brother screamed, 'You leave her alone.'"

Marie's brother became the target of their father's rage. With supper dishes flying, Marie's dad shoved the table and her brother across the kitchen floor. To this day, a dropped dish makes Marie want to run out of the room.

"I remember my brother flat against the wall with my dad pushing the table against his neck. I thought he was going to kill him. Mom started screaming and hitting him. Then he grabbed her by the hair and dragged her into the bedroom."

Marie then divulged a secret she had guarded for over sixty years. "My brother and I sat crying on the kitchen floor while we heard

Dad in the next room forcing my mom to have sex with him." Marie then confided with a blend of naïveté and surprise, "Do you know that affected my sex life when I got married?"

Thankfully, Marie was blessed with a gentle and patient husband. His tenderness taught Marie that sexual touch could be sacred and beautiful, which was God's intent.

The Value of Touch

There is indescribable power in a father's touch. His hands can bring a blessing or cast a curse. The memory of a father's touch can either be an ever-present source of affirmation or a continual cause of anxiety. For better or worse, a father's touch lays the groundwork for his children's future relationships.

Ray knows well the value of human touch. More appropriately, he understands the ache of *not* receiving positive touch from his dad. Ray was born of an unwed mother and a father who, despite Ray's efforts, remains anonymous. After being labeled an "inconvenience" by his mother, Ray was adopted by parents who were not as interested in having a son as they were a dependent to claim on their taxes.

Ray longed to one day give to his children the nurturing that he never received, but after fourteen years of marriage, dozens of consultations with doctors, and thousands of dollars spent on fertilization treatments, Ray and his wife remained childless.

As a form of therapy to help him deal with his sadness, as well as providing an outlet for his need to bless little ones with the gift of touch, Ray, every Saturday, drives thirty miles to a hospital in Chicago where he volunteers as a baby cuddler. Many neonatal hospitals, nurseries, and orphanages enlist volunteers like Ray to simply hold babies and young children who do not have adequate human contact early in life.

Some of the little ones Ray cradles in his arms have been abandoned by their parents. Many are the children of parents who have

115

been assigned to drug rehab. Most are babies born prematurely who need to remain in the hospital until they are strong enough to go home. Holding these little ones helps satisfy Ray's longing to bless children with a gift he never received. Although he finds it incomprehensible, all receive more from Ray's embrace than he does.

Robbed

Wayne, a philanthropist from the Midwest, has always had a warm place in his heart for orphaned children. Having been adopted himself after being abandoned by his parents he saw to it that the financial needs of the local orphanage were met. Wanting the kids to have a homey environment at Christmas time, he anonymously donated a truckload of Christmas decorations to the orphanage. The intended centerpiece was a waving mechanical Santa.

Just before Christmas, Wayne visited the orphanage with a church group to bring presents and sing carols for the kids. The mechanical Santa was conspicuously absent. He knew it would compromise his anonymity, but he pulled the orphanage director aside and asked why all the decorations were not displayed. The director's explanation as to Santa's whereabouts left him sick to his stomach.

Wayne was told that the children had all gathered around excitedly when Santa was taken out of the box. Their limited experience with jolly, old St. Nick assured them that he was a safe figure. He had to be if kids were willing to crawl up in his lap at the mall. But once the mechanical Santa was plugged in and raised his hand to wave, several of the children ran out of the room, many in tears. In their experience, a raised hand only meant one thing. They were about to be beaten.

In their experience, a raised hand only meant one thing. They were about to be beaten.

Many of us have been robbed of the loving touch of a father. Some grew up with dads who were abusive. Others had fathers who, for various reasons, were absent. Some had dads who simply didn't know how to give the gift of touch to their kids because they never received it when they were young. All have missed out on a very special blessing that was part of God's original plan for all of His children.

God's Gift

Loving touch is an intricately designed gift from our Heavenly Father. When God meticulously crafted us in our mothers' wombs, the first sense He developed in us was the sense of touch. By the time we were born God had wired five million touch receptors in our bodies, over one-third of them in our hands. We are designed by our Creator in such a way that human touch is not only essential to our *thriving*, it is essential to our *surviving*.

Touch is vital to the health and development of all human beings, regardless of age. Just like food and water, touch is a basic human need. Dr. Fritz Talbot, during a visit to a children's clinic in the 1940s, discovered an irrefutable connection between touch and a baby's ability to survive. He observed how babies who were sick and were not responding to conventional medical treatment began to rally when they were regularly held and touched.

In the 1960s, psychologist Harry Frederick Harlow conducted a series of experiments using rhesus monkeys to determine the effects of social isolation. Some monkeys were subjected to partial isolation. They were placed in wire cages that allowed them to see, smell, and hear other monkeys without being allowed physical contact with them. The result: The touch-deprived monkeys developed a number of abnormalities including repetitious circling in the cage, blank staring, and self-mutilation.

Monkeys that were totally isolated for a minimum of three months showed irreversible psychological problems. Upon re-entering a normal social setting, these monkeys would, in most cases, go into a state of emotional shock characterized by rocking and self-clutching. An autopsy report on one monkey that died upon re-entry to the community concluded that the cause of death was "emotional anorexia." [13]

God created every one of us with a need to touch and be touched. The benefits of human touch are well documented. Studies have shown that positive touch offers these physiological benefits:

- Reduced stress

- Improved brain chemistry

- Stimulation of the release of serotonin which counteracts pain

- Increased ability to cope

- Slowed heart rate

- Lowered blood pressure

- Facilitation of the digestive process

- Increased immune cells

One study has even shown that hugging can lower a person's cholesterol—a much more appealing alternative than taking Lipitor and cutting out fried foods.

Healthy, loving human touch, however, radiates beyond the physical body. Touch, as God intended, embraces the soul. There is a deeply spiritual benefit to touch, particularly when given from a father to his child.

There is a deeply spiritual benefit to touch, particularly when given from a father to his child.

A Father's Touch

A father's touch is simply not the same as a mother's physical expressions of love. There is something about a father's touch that is different. Our culture views the ideal mother as a tender nurturer and the model father as a strong provider. As a result, while many of us have grown up reveling in hugs and kisses from a mom, we see her actions as more or less expected. But the loving embrace of a father, the gentle touch of the one who created us, tends to speak more to our soul.

- A father's touch expresses a deeper level of affection.

- A father's touch conveys a stronger sense of worth.

- A father's touch, like none other, affirms a child's value.

- A father's touch helps build a child's bonds with God.

- A father's touch molds lives.

Jesus's Touch

In biblical times, touch was essential to convey love and compassion. Jesus modeled this wonderfully.

It is said there are two types of people in the world: those who are touchy-feely and those who are not. Those in "Group A" go through life freely seeking to share God's gift of touch by patting, cuddling, squeezing, holding, hugging, and high-fiving everyone they can get their hands on. Those in "Group B" group spend much of their lives trying to avoid those in "Group A."

There is strong biblical evidence that Jesus was in "Group A." Since He could do all things, He had the power to heal people without even being in the same hemisphere, let alone the same room. But because He also knew all things, He most certainly understood the value of being on the receiving end of touch. The Bible records a number of occasions when Jesus met people where they were, one-on-one, so that He could offer hands-on healing.

The book of Mark includes three stories—all involving the touch of Jesus— that have found their way into most Sunday School curricula. But there is a lesson in each that is often overlooked. In that gospel we read, "A man with leprosy came and knelt in front of Jesus, begging to be healed. 'If you are willing, you can heal me and make me clean,' he said. Moved with compassion, Jesus reached out and touched him. 'I am willing,' he said. 'Be healed!' Instantly the leprosy disappeared, and the man was healed" (Mark 1:40–42, NLT).

There is a profundity in this interaction that is easily missed. There was no obvious reason why Jesus had to touch this man and a long list of reasons why He shouldn't have.

Leprosy is a highly contagious disease. In the days of Jesus, those who were afflicted were not only banned from communal religious activity, but also prohibited from all physical contact. Think about that. No pecks on their wife's cheek as they left for work in the morning. No goodnight hugs as their kids went off to bed. No handshakes when they met up with friends on the street. Lepers were forced to live on the outskirts of town to prevent their physical interaction with others. If anyone even walked in their direction, lepers had to warn him or her by yelling out, "Unclean! Unclean!" Not only were lepers considered unclean, not only were they banished from family and community life, so was anyone who touched them.

Clearly, Jesus's touch was not necessary to bring healing to the man's body, but it *was* essential to bring healing to his soul.

When the leprous man knelt before Him, Jesus could have healed him by snapping His fingers. He could have restored him to health with the twitch of His nose or the touch of a divine wand. Those certainly would have been more socially acceptable methods for the healing of a leper. What makes Jesus's encounter with the leper so incredible is found in an often overlooked phrase in the middle of the story: *Jesus reached out and touched him.* Jesus saw a deeper need in this man.

And He tenderly met it. Clearly, Jesus's touch was not necessary to bring healing to the man's body, but it *was* essential to bring healing to his soul. In the simple, yet intentional act of placing His hands on the leper, Jesus replaced stigma with significance; He traded disgrace for grace. He freed the man to experience the touch of loved ones once again.

Validated

A few chapters after Mark wrote of Jesus's encounter with the leper, he tells this story:

"And a woman was there who had been subject to bleeding for twelve years. She had suffered a great deal under the care of many doctors and had spent all she had, yet instead of getting better she grew worse. When she heard about Jesus, she came up behind him in the crowd and touched his cloak, because she thought, 'If I just touch his clothes, I will be healed.' Immediately her bleeding stopped and she felt in her body that she was freed from her suffering. At once Jesus realized that power had gone out from Him. He turned around in the crowd and asked, 'Who touched my clothes?'

"'You see the people crowding against you,' his disciples answered, 'and yet you can ask, Who touched me?' But Jesus kept looking around to see who had done it.

Then the woman, knowing what had happened to her, came and fell at his feet and, trembling with fear, told him the whole truth. He said to her, 'Daughter, your faith has healed you. Go in peace and be freed from your suffering'" (Mark 5:25–34, NIV).

A crucial detail in this story is that Jesus's run-in with this woman took place as He was making His way to the home of a synagogue ruler named Jairus. Jairus had met up with Jesus in the midst of a crowd and "When he saw Jesus, he fell at his feet, pleading fervently with him. 'My little daughter is dying,' he said. 'Please come and lay your hands on her; heal her so she can live'" (Mark 5:22–23, NLT).

Jesus's entourage saw this as major photo op. Jairus was an important person; well-known and well-respected. He was a somebody. Certainly Jesus's healing his daughter was going to get a lot of press. But while on His way to what was sure to be a media event that would garner Him headlines in the Galilee Gazette Jesus was sidetracked by a sickly woman.

Years earlier, just about the time Jairus and Mrs. Jairus sent out birth announcements of their new baby girl, this woman set out to visit her doctor to seek help for some abnormal bleeding. Twelve years and several doctors later, the bleeding continued. Complicating her physical condition was her subsequent social status. According to the rules of ritual purity she was considered unclean. It was with desperation and faith that she reached out for the healing touch of Jesus.

She surged forward with the crowd, her arms extended beyond their normal reach. She hoped for physical contact, however slight, with the Healer. With her window of opportunity closing quickly she lunged toward Jesus. She missed, but she did manage, for a split second, to touch His garment. That was enough. In that instant she knew she was healed. She could feel it. And so could Jesus.

Mission seemingly accomplished, He could have kept walking. But Jesus had a deeper mission.

Jesus stopped and asked, "Who touched my clothes?" Do we seriously think the all-seeing, all-knowing Son of God didn't know who touched Him? We find out from the story that Jesus looked around to see who did it. For the woman it was like trying to hide in an empty parking lot. Yet, frozen with guilt, she didn't fess up.

The Teacher had called her out, but it wasn't to make her feel ashamed. It was to take her shame away.

For an unclean woman to touch a rabbi was beyond a

cultural faux pas. And for her to speak in public to any man, let alone the Son of Man, was preposterous. When it became obvious that Jesus was prepared to wait for a confession, she stepped forward. The Teacher had called her out, but it wasn't to make her feel ashamed. It was to take her shame away.

When Jesus then invited her to share her story surely there were those in the crowd, not the least of whom was Jairus, who weren't the least bit interested in this distraction. After all, the real story was the healing of Jairus's daughter. But by taking the time to listen to this woman's pain, Jesus gave her something she hadn't bargained for; something she hadn't had for twelve years—dignity. His undivided attentiveness to her real need validated her worth as a child of the Heavenly Father.

Her touching His cloak had already brought about healing from her outer bleeding, but Jesus could see that the much greater issue was her internal bleeding. It was only after He had healed the wounds on the inside caused by twelve years of embarrassment and abandonment that He said, "Daughter, your faith has healed you. Go in peace and be freed from your suffering."

Untold Blessing

The third story of Jesus's touch found in the book of Mark may be the most alarming, particularly in our current culture: "One day some parents brought their children to Jesus so he could touch and bless them. But the disciples scolded the parents for bothering Him. When Jesus saw what was happening, he was angry with his disciples. He said to them, 'Let the children come to me. Don't stop them! For the Kingdom of God belongs to those who are like these children. I tell you the truth, anyone who doesn't receive the Kingdom of God like a child will never enter it.' Then he took the children in his arms and placed his hands on their heads and blessed them" (Mark 10:13–16, NLT).

Just a few short years ago, the part of this story that would be considered most disturbing was the disciples' response. They tried to keep the children away from Jesus. But today, many people wouldn't be able to get past the first sentence of this story. *Parents would actually bring their children to Jesus so He could touch them?* Appalling. The tragically frequent incidences of inappropriate touch involving children and authority figures, particularly in church settings, have rendered us a touch-phobic society.

We live in a time when more and more schools and nurseries are instituting "no touch" policies, due to fear of allegations of abuse. In some schools teachers cannot put a Band-Aid on a child without parental consent. Many nurseries are requiring employees to keep logs of all incidents that involve physical contact of any kind with a child. In several daycares across the country, even picking up a crying child requires detailed documentation of the time it took place and the circumstances around it.

I recently read a newspaper account of a male gym teacher who had to leave an injured girl in the hallway so he could get a female colleague in case she would have to be repositioned to relieve her pain, necessitating she be touched.

Perhaps some of you who are reading this book have been the victims of a father's physical or sexual abuse. You may shudder at the thought of parents bringing their children to a strange rabbi so he could touch them. But in biblical times, meaningful, physical touch was imperative in the passing of a blessing from one person to another. Blessings could not be imparted without the blesser touching the blessee. It was the act of touch—whether a kiss, an embrace, or the laying on of hands—that conveyed acceptance, warmth, and affirmation.

It was the act of touch—whether a kiss, an embrace, or the laying on of hands—that conveyed acceptance, warmth, and affirmation.

Parents in Jesus's day took note that *His* touch, in particular, was a source of untold blessing. So like parents do today with Santa Claus at the mall, moms and dads lined up where Jesus was seated and waited so their children could have lap time. Parents yearned for Jesus's holy, healing hands of blessing to rest on their little ones.

However, in the story told by James, the disciples got a bit zealous in their crowd-control efforts. They demanded adherence to the social protocol of the day: Children should be seen and not heard. They scolded the parents for wasting Jesus's valuable time with a bunch of little ankle-biters. Jesus responded by reprimanding the disciples: "Let the children come to me. Don't stop them! For the Kingdom of God belongs to those who are like these children." Again, by giving His undivided attention to those whom that society gave little value, Jesus affirmed every child's personhood. Every one of God's children were and are important to Him.

Can't you just picture Jesus with those little ones? Looking into the face of an infant cradled in His arms, making funny goo-goo sounds, trying to coax a smile. Blowing zerberts on a toddler's chubby cheek. Getting kids to squeal in laughter with a playful poke or a good-natured noogie.

With the mere touch of His hand, Jesus validated the significance of those His culture deemed insignificant. Being both fully human and fully divine, He taught the importance of both human touch and divine touch. Today, we too are blessed by both—even more so in the absence of a father's touch.

Craving Touch

For some of us, receiving the gift of loving touch from our dads is just a memory. Our dads are no longer around. It is very common in the grieving process, no matter what the reason for the separation, to crave our father's touch, especially when it once served as a source of blessing and affirmation.

In the 1970s (which I contend was the best decade for music ever), a group called Bread recorded a song called "Everything I Own." The song seemed to fit into a rather popular genre of pop music—songs about hearts broken by lost love.

Indeed, "Everything I Own" is a song about lost love, but not of the romantic variety. Now that I know the story behind the song, I feel an emotional wallop every time I hear it. Contrary to what many baby boomers believed, Bread's hit song is not about a guy mourning his best girl breaking up with him. The group's lead singer, David Gates, wrote the lyrics when dealing with a very different kind of loss—the death of his father. Rather than a trite ditty written about a changed Facebook status, the song is a grateful tribute penned in response to a changed life.

You sheltered me from harm, kept me warm, kept me warm
You gave my life to me; set me free, set me free
The finest years I ever knew were all the years I had with you

And I would give anything I own, I'd give up my life, my heart, my home
I would give everything I own just to have you back again.

You taught me how to love, what it's of, what it's of
You never said too much but still you showed the way
And I knew, from watching you
Nobody else will ever know the part of me that can't let go

I would give anything I own, I'd give up my life, my heart, my home
I will give everything I own just to have you back again

Is there someone you know, you're loving them so
But taking them all for granted
You may lose them one day, someone takes them away
And they don't hear the words you long to say

I would give anything I own, I'd give up my life, my heart, my home,
I will give everything I own just to have you back again
Just to touch you once again [14]

In His Lap

A few weeks after my dad died, I found myself reverting back to self-protective patterns I developed very early in life. But while isolating myself when in a hurtful situation was helpful when I was a child, it proved harmful to me as an adult.

The number of people I allowed into my inner circle could be counted on one hand. My friend Rich was the middle finger. He was rough and gruff. As true friends do, he often said things that needed to be said when I didn't want to hear them. But under that prickly exterior was a tender and loving heart. Rich was compassionately confrontational. When my attitude and behavior threatened my well-being, he stood gloved and gowned, scalpel in hand, ready to provide the needed spiritual surgery.

On this particular day, Rich correctly perceived that I was not only bearing the weight of the loss of my dad, I was also grieving the loss of my childhood. Rich listened to all I had to say. But, with his keen insight, he also heard what I didn't say. He sensed that the little boy inside me was mourning the loss of a close relationship with his dad. So he stretched out one of his big arms and wrapped it around my shoulder. He pulled me close enough to feel the whiskers of his goatee on my cheek and said, "Sounds to me like you need to crawl up in God's lap for a while and just let Him love on you."

Though my spontaneous tears indicated how much I needed to do just that, it took me a while to fill that prescription. I first had to **Now there is no place I would rather be than in the arms of my Heavenly Father.** allow myself to be vulnerable enough to assume such a position. Once I came to the point where I could trust that my Heavenly

Father really did love me, I held out my arms and let Him pull me up. Now there is no place I would rather be than in the arms of my Heavenly Father.

Experience His Embrace

Naysayers may ask, *how can you experience the embrace of a God who isn't a physical being?* Very simply, it's through the development of another of God's amazing gifts: the gift of imagination. Our imaginations allow us to instantly be anywhere at any time. Conjuring up images in our head of pleasant places or experiences can bring peace and relaxation, not just to our minds, but to our bodies and souls.

Jan and I have often visited family members and friends in Arizona. How anyone can live in Arizona, surrounded every day with scenery so serene, so splendorous, and not palpably experience the presence of God is beyond me. The sight of brilliant red rock formations freckled with majestic saguaros set against a cloudless, azure sky ushers me right into God's presence. Granted, we always go to Arizona in March when the temperature is heavenly. In August the desert is more the devil's domain.

There is a mountain in Arizona my wife and I like to climb after we've had our morning coffee. Locals would call it a foothill but we Hoosiers know a mountain when we see it. Near its peak is a flat-topped boulder-for-two with Creator-carved butt grooves where Jan and I sit in silence and simply take in the majesty and wonder of God. "God Mountain," as we call it, has become for us a symbol of rest and renewal.

I cannot, on a writer's wages, visit Arizona as much as I would like. But utilizing God's wonderful gift of imagination, I can be atop God Mountain in an instant without having to endure three hours in a plane and four hours filling out paperwork at Hertz. No matter where in the world I am, I can escape the memories of the past and the mess of the present simply by visualizing that view from God Mountain. When I close my eyes and place myself on that hill, I find that my pulse slows, my blood pressure stabilizes, and my breathing settles back into my belly.

The power of imagination can unleash in us God's creative powers to transform our reality, even bringing us hope in the midst of seemingly hopeless situations. Dr. Frank Lawlis in his book *The Stress Answer* writes, "Imagery has been shown to have very promising benefits for chronic pain, especially back pain, and has also been found to have some measureable, positive therapeutic effects for autoimmune diseases such as arthritis and even for cancer."

> The power of imagination can unleash in us God's creative powers to transform our reality, even bringing us hope in the midst of seemingly hopeless situations.

Everyone possesses imagination ability. However, we don't often use our imagination to its fullest. Some may have no problem coming up with *visual* images, but in order to receive the full benefits of imagination, it is important that we use *all* of our senses.

It's easy, for example, to close our eyes and visualize our favorite vacation spot. If that vacation is of the tropical variety, we can readily picture in our minds the white sand beach, the palm trees, the turquoise water, and the cloudless sky; but a sharpened imagination calls all of our senses into play. When we engage every sense, we can then hear the waves splash onto the shore and the sandpipers chirp at each other as they forage for food at the waterfront. We can smell the freshness of the ocean breeze, colored by the scent of cocoa butter sunscreen and the aroma of tropical flowers. We can taste the coconut in our fruit smoothie and the berry flavor in our lip balm. We feel the wisp of a wind rolling across our sweat-glistened body and the tiny grains of sand wedged in our toes. By training our imagination we are able to utilize all of our senses.

When I spend time in God's lap, I imagine myself as being a young boy, maybe five or six years old. I picture God as Jesus, the human form of Himself. I feel His rugged yet tender hand on the side of my face as He gently holds my head against His chest. His linen garment has a distinctly musky masculine smell, yet has captured the alluring scent of wildflowers and wheat. I loosely grasp His wrist, rubbing my fingers over the soft hairs on His forearm and circling my thumb over the rough, round scar on His wrist. I am enchanted by the strong, steady beat of His heart, which my ear can both hear and feel. Safe and serene, calmed in His caress, I am lost in the love of my Father.

I now regularly take the time to experience my Heavenly Father's embrace. Yet, for many, this imagery so quickens our pulse and shortens our breath it's as if we're about to encounter Jason of *Friday the Thirteenth* fame. Our past experience with this kind of closeness—especially from one called *father*—has only led to us being hurt.

I have met people who were subjected to physical and/or sexual abuse at the hand of their fathers who often want nothing to do with a male God. The thought of being in a Heavenly Father's lap terrifies them. So in a self-protective and well-rehearsed maneuver, they cut themselves off from God. But what they don't often realize is that severing our relationship with the Heavenly Father effectively stops the flow of healing and wholeness in our lives. When we turn our backs on God, we are rejecting the only One who can give us what we desperately seek.

If the thought of placing yourself in the embrace of your Heavenly Father stirs up anything but thoughts of perfect serenity and overwhelming love then your impressions of Him are flawed.

Get your highlighter ready for the rest of this paragraph. If the thought of placing yourself in the embrace of your Heavenly Father stirs up anything but thoughts of perfect serenity and overwhelming love then your impressions of Him are flawed. For our souls to be restored and our spirits renewed, we must find out who He is. Not who we think He is. Not who misinformed parents or misguided preachers tell us He is. We must find out who He *really* is.

Rembrandt's *Father*

My favorite story from Scripture was told by Jesus and is commonly known as the parable of the prodigal son. The abridged version of the parable is this: A son asks for an early inheritance, leaves home, blows his money on wild living, then comes back home where he is greeted with open arms by his father and with folded arms by his older brother. The story is one of my favorites, primarily because it is the story of a father's love.

In 1662, Rembrandt captured the meaning of this parable, as he saw it, in his painting *The Return of the Prodigal Son*. The representation depicts the younger son on his knees before his father; disheveled, clothes tattered, sandal missing. In the father's eyes and in his embrace, Rembrandt poignantly captures the depth of this father's love for his boy. But using a zoom lens on this picture reveals an apparent error that may suggest Rembrandt finished the painting after finishing more than a few Heinekens. The father's hands, placed by Rembrandt on the prodigal son's back, don't appear to belong to the same person. The right hand is noticeably different from the left. The mismatched mitts were intentional. Rembrandt gave the father figure a man's hand and a woman's hand.

The left hand is a father's hand. It is clearly masculine. The fingers are rugged and muscular. They are spread out on the son's shoulder. The hand is painted in such a way that it symbolizes strength and security. Placed on the boy's shoulder, the hand seems to fortify more than touch. The right hand is a mother's hand. Obviously feminine, the long, slender fingers are close together and suggest warmth, gentleness, and tenderness. By placing the right hand on the center of the boy's back the artist portrayed support and affirmation.

In his subtle style, Rembrandt brilliantly captures the all-encompassing love of our Heavenly Father: strong yet sensitive, protecting yet pacifying, confirming yet compassionate.

The touch of our Heavenly Father is unlike any human touch we have ever experienced.

The touch of our Heavenly Father is unlike any human touch we have ever experienced. Climbing up into His lap and allowing ourselves to experience that touch may not come easy. It may take a great deal of emotional effort. It may require a deeper level of vulnerability and trust than we are comfortable with. One voice inside us may tell us it's okay while another warns us to stay away. It is important that we honor both voices. The latter voice may have served us well in the past. In adolescence it may have protected us from dangerous situations. But now in adulthood we hear a new voice; a voice that says, *I'm stronger now. I'm ready to risk. I need to open myself up to the love of this Father.*

We must not dismiss either voice, but respect each, then make a decision about which voice to follow. In time, and with the Heavenly Father's help, we will get beyond *knowing* what the Scriptures tell us about Him and will reach the point of *believing* what is true about Him. Once we begin *believing* the truth—that He is loving and compassionate; that He readily forgives our sins, even when we can't forgive ourselves; that He treasures us more than anything; that He delights to hold us in His arms—we can then *experience* the warmth of His touch. When we fully comprehend that we can trust Him it will only be a matter of time before we find ourselves safe in His arms, lost in His love.

There is healing and blessing in His touch. There was with the leper. There was with the bleeding woman. There was with the little children who were brought before Him. There is with you and me.

CHAPTER 8

A Father Who Encourages Us

Words have a longer life than deeds.

Pindar, Greek lyric poet

I am one of those rare birds who would rather write a book than read one. I'm getting better. I'm reading a lot more in my adult years, but I would still prefer to wait until the movie comes out.

Reading a book and actually comprehending its message is next to impossible in a house with an alcoholic in residence. In the home I grew up in, the moments of peace and calm were eerie; like the stillness that hovers moments before a tornado—an atmosphere not exactly conducive to trying to follow a storyline in a book. Maybe it's because writing requires more concentration that I find it easier.

Although I did not complete most of my reading assignments, I did fairly well in school because I had the detestable yet enviable ability to write creatively on subjects I knew precious little about. My classmates in high school gave me the stink eye when I would ace book reports on books I never read. I had a BS in b.s. What can I say? It's a gift.

I've always been fascinated by words. I enjoy playing games that have to do with words. Through the years I have won millions of dollars in cash and prizes playing *Wheel of Fortune* from the privacy of my living room. Granted, it's much easier to play the game without the pressure of live competition. Not to mention the fact that when you play along at home it's always your turn. My family refuses to watch *Wheel* with me because I shout out the answer before they or the contestants can. To ease the family tension my wife pries the remote from my fingers at six o'clock and turns on *Everybody Loves Raymond*. Just for the record, not everybody does.

Boggle is another game that puts me at odds with my loved ones. Jan has a gift for finding all the obscure, little words that only English teachers and voracious readers could identify as legitimate words (like *tam, lee,* and *sot*). But while she wastes time with all her measly one-pointers I tend to shoot from beyond the three-point line. The conflict arises when she challenges me on whether certain words I have written down are actually words. I think she's just being persnicious (an eight-pointer—hah!).

Although I do pretty well at filling in missing letters and finding words in a puzzle, I am in awe of people blessed with the ability to rearrange the letters of words to come up with other words. This talent is particularly astounding when there's irony involved. For instance, did you know that when you juggle the letters in the word *astronomer* you can get *moon starer*? How cool is that?

Other favorite anagrams due to their ironic nature include:

- *the eyes = they see*

- *eleven plus two = twelve plus one*

- *dormitory = dirty room*

- *slot machines = cash lost in me*

You don't even need to rearrange the letters to turn *The IRS* into *theirs*. Words can be so much fun.

According to Wikipedia (the source of all truth that isn't God), the average adult speaks sixteen thousand words a day. Contrary to what the male population may believe, no, the number of words spoken per day by women is not three times the number spoken by men. Studies conclude it is roughly the same.

According to the source of all truth that *is* God, it is important that we be discerning about the words we choose to use. That's because words carry a great deal of power. Our words have the potential to build people up or to tear them down. Our words can fill others with confidence or drain them of it. Our words can be a source of *en*couragement or *dis*couragement.

Words That Give Courage

The simple definition of *encouragement* is *to give courage to*. God has given fathers the responsibility to give courage to their children. Many of them fail miserably. Rather than equipping their children to be confident with comments like *attaboy, attagirl, I'm proud of you, great job,* many fathers thwart their kids' emotional development with remarks like *what's wrong with you, grow up already, you are such a disappointment,* and even *I wish you were never born.*

> **God has given fathers the responsibility to give courage to their children.**

A golden nugget in the book of Proverbs offers this truth: "Reckless words pierce like a sword, but the tongue of the wise brings healing" (Prov. 12:18, NIV). It's *how* we use our words that makes a difference in others—for good or bad. The same principle applies to using a knife. In the hands of a skilled surgeon, a knife can facilitate healing, but in the hands of someone who is careless (or clueless) it can cause irreparable damage.

I once attended a holiday gathering where a little girl, maybe six or seven years old, was carrying her food into the next room when her balance shifted, her glass of milk slid across the plastic tray, and with a startling crash the tray with everything on it landed on the kitchen floor. The second the dishes hit the linoleum her father yelled from across the kitchen, "June! How can you be so stupid?" It wasn't the embarrassment of the accident that made June sob. It was being humiliated by her father's words. She fell to her knees, weeping, her hands over her face—an image I will never forget. Those of us who were standing nearby quickly knelt to help her clean up the broken dishes, but we were helpless to fix her broken spirit. If I, as a mere bystander, can still vividly recall the incident, I can only imagine that it hasn't escaped June's memory. June may still find herself trying to clean up the mess made by her father's caustic and careless words. Humiliation in the hands of our *enemies* may cut us deep, but being humiliated by our own father can cause wounds that never heal.

Reckless Words

When our son was in grade school he played on a little league team with a boy whose father was the manager. As many coach/dads are inclined to believe, Mike was of the brazenly biased opinion that his son was the best player on the team. In this case, it was actually true. Mike's son was a phenomenal athlete. Ricky was voted to the all-star team by the other managers every season. His face was easily imagined on a baseball card.

Ricky was one of those boys who developed much faster than other boys his age. While I am in my fifties and still have trouble growing facial hair, Ricky had sideburns at age eleven. He stood a foot taller than the rest of the boys on the team. He was a man-child.

When he swung a baseball bat, he looked like Herman Munster, except without the flat head and bolts sticking out of his neck. In addition to his offensive prowess, Ricky was also an excellent fielder. He exhibited natural instincts when playing the field. His skill with a first baseman's glove saved the other infielders countless errors as he scooped their would-be errant throws out of the dirt.

That is why it was such a surprise when once, in the early innings of a game, on what should have been an easy play, Ricky dropped a perfect throw from the shortstop, allowing a run to score. Ricky's father slammed his three-ring binder to the ground and bolted out of the dugout. He stormed toward his son, jerked his thumb into the air, and yelled, "Get off the field!" Ricky was mortified. He held his ground in disbelief as his father motioned for one of the boys on the bench to take over at first. It wasn't until his replacement arrived that Ricky realized his father was serious. Ricky hung his head and slinked off the field with his dad within kicking distance, spewing loud enough for people in the concession stand to hear, "You can't even catch a ball. And you call yourself an All-Star?"

Reckless words pierce like a sword, indeed.

How I wish I could have stepped into Ricky's life at that moment, given his dad the thumb and screamed, "And you call yourself a father?"

Sticks and Stones

To put to rest once and for all an old childhood adage, words *can* hurt us. Comedian Eric Idle (of Monty Python fame) once said, "Sticks and stones may break my bones, but words will make me go in a corner and cry by myself for hours."

We are so careless with our words in our culture today. Daytime

> To put to rest once and for all an old childhood adage, words *can* hurt us.

talk shows promote confrontation and humiliation as acceptable forms of communication. What's even more disturbing than people carving each other up with their words on national television is that millions of people derive some sort of pleasure from watching it. The political world has always been a hotbed of reckless words. How shameful that there are good, upstanding, moral people who decline the opportunity to run for public office only because they fear what will be said about them and their family. Today's media is more bent on finding dirt than an obsessive-compulsive housewife with a Dustbuster. The younger generation is learning well from us adults. Bullying has become an epidemic in our country. Making the problem more tragic is that the spiteful, malicious words of bullies are no longer confined to the playground. Young children and teens today use electronic devices to broadcast hateful messages about people they don't like—messages for all the world to read, words that can never be taken back.

"Words can never hurt me?" Think again.

While walking down the hallway after speaking at an elementary school about the pain our words can cause others, I was approached by a teacher named Chris. Chris confirmed my message, but not in terms of how it impacted her students. She tearfully recalled how when she was in sixth grade, the girls in her class formed an "I hate Chris" club. More than ten years later, this teacher's heart was still pierced by the words of those girls; words which continued to replay at full volume in her mind.

With the fallout of careless words all around us, it becomes that much more important that our homes be havens, where the words spoken are nurturing, affirming, and encouraging.

Darlene's Dilemma

Darlene sat silently in the car with her husband and children. She watched as her father's casket was carried out of the church by men she didn't know and placed in the back of the black hearse. All the while, she shook her head in disbelief—not that her father had died, but that the pastor had lied. The reverend's funeral message depicted her deceased dad as a true family man: a man who was there for his kids, a man who was a constant source of encouragement to them, a man who was committed to helping his children succeed in life. Unfortunately, it was a man she never knew.

Darlene's parents, Rob and Patty, divorced when she was just a teen. What she remembered most about her father was that he was hard to love. He had the uncanny ability to make people feel insignificant without saying a word; he could be condescending with his eyes. To his family, he was both hypercritical and hypocritical—an unfortunate combination that stripped him of all integrity. He would pat people on the back in public after stabbing them in the back in private. While Darlene was still in grade school she had already assessed the situation with the precision of a masters level therapist: Her father, much like a grade school bully, had zero self-worth and could only make himself feel better by constantly putting others down.

Darlene remembers that whenever she engaged in a verbal altercation with her father he would brandish his favorite firearm; a weapon that was sure to put her in her place, immobilizing her with recurrent pangs of guilt. He would mercilessly pelt her with the word "*should*"—*You should know better. You should do as I say. You should study harder. You should have made those free throws. You should appreciate all I've done for you.*

The word wounded Darlene's mom as well—*You should shut up and mind your own business. You should realize how good you've got it. If you want to know what the problem is you should look in the mirror.*

Rob once smugly walked away from an argument after blasting his wife with, *You should just leave if you're so unhappy.* He wasn't quite so smug when she took him up on it. She took the kids and left. She told Rob she wasn't coming back until he agreed to see a counselor. He found that stipulation laughable. After all, *he* wasn't the one with the problem.

It was less than a year after the divorce when Rob found a new wife and children. After a fifteen-year reign of terror over his first family, he shamelessly substituted another. He married a single mom with two small children. But this time things were different. Perhaps it was because he had learned from his mistakes, perhaps it was to heap burning coals on his ex-wife's head, but, judging from the way he spoke to and treated his new family, it appeared he was a changed man. Rob treated his new wife like a queen. He spent more time playing with his new kids than he ever did with his own children. His makeover proved cosmetic. Once his replacement family was in position Rob stopped all communication with his first family.

Not only did he begin attending church regularly with his new family, he became quite involved. His pastor, observing Rob's loving interaction with his new wife and children, encouraged him to participate in the church's caring ministries. Rob soon had the reputation among his church friends of being a warm and genuine man who put his family first, yet still took time to reach out to those in need.

Rob's new family, new pastor, and new friends were unaware of his old ways. They never saw his *before* picture, only the *after*. So when Rob died unexpectedly of a brain aneurism and his pastor had to deliver the eulogy, he wasn't intentionally creating a fictional character, as clergy sometimes do, in an effort to make the deceased sound holier than he or she really was. The pastor spoke honestly about the man he knew. It's just that the loving family man he spoke of was not a part of Darlene's reality. Darlene not only buried her father that day. She buried an ideal.

Should

Darlene was beaten down by one of the most *dis*couraging words in the English language—*should*. It is a word that can poison a relationship—particularly a father/child relationship. *Should* is a word that points a finger in our face and scolds us for not measuring up. *Should* implies dissatisfaction caused by unmet expectations.

> **Should is a word that points a finger in our face and scolds us for not measuring up.**

Should casts judgment. *Should* has connotations of superiority, even arrogance, reducing to peon status those on the receiving end. *Should* should be banned from our homes.

Habitual use of the word is straight out abusive. The toxins in that combination of six letters ooze into our souls. And when it's used often enough by others to beat us down we become prone to punch ourselves with it.

Years ago, the thinking was that anyone who talked to themselves was destined for a straightjacket and a rubber room. In point of fact, we all talk to ourselves. It's actually healthy. That renowned philosopher A. Nonymous once said, "The most important opinion you have is the one you have of yourself, and the most significant things you say all day are those things you say to yourself." But while self-talk can be beneficial it proves dangerous when our words are not controlled. Using the word *should* on ourselves; incessantly telling ourselves that we *should* be better, bigger, smarter, stronger, healthier, or holier than we are can lead us to conclude that we are worthless, or, worse yet, hopeless.

Like steel-toed work boots on an Olympic pole-vaulter, self-imposed *shoulds* weigh us down. They prevent us from clearing the standards we set for ourselves. Darlene found herself unable to get off the ground. Years after being "should" on by her father Darlene was "shoulding" on herself. *You should be handling this better. You should be over this by now. You should be grateful for the good relationships you have.* *Should*s directed inward are a form of self-abuse.

A God Who "Shoulds"

The consequences of a *should* mindset can be devastating. When we become accustomed to others using the word on us and when we, in turn, abuse ourselves with it, it's easy to imagine it being part of our Heavenly Father's vocabulary as well: *You should go to church more. You should pray more. You should be ashamed.*

When these are the kinds of messages we hear from God, it makes sense that we would conclude that we will never meet His expectations; that we have no right to feel good about ourselves; that there truly is no hope for us. Our concept of God becomes that of a never-satisfied parent; looking over the top of His glasses at us with a furrowed brow, shaking His head as He lectures us with an endless litany of *you should*s.

If we are carrying around with us this snapshot of God we are assured that we will live in a continual state of disgrace. But the Bible assures us that God has a much more uplifting message that He wants to convey to His children. He speaks words to us that *en*courage, not *dis*courage. He longs to build us up when He communicates with us, not tear us down. He is all about freedom from shame, not bondage to it.

The Power of Encouragement

Check out this jewel from the book of Proverbs: "Pleasant words are like honey—sweet to the soul and healthy for the body" (Prov. 16:24, NLT). Did you get that? Encouraging words are not only pleasant to our ears, they are beneficial to us *spiritually and physically*!

Encouraging words are not only pleasant to our ears, they are beneficial to us *spiritually and physically*!

Stop right now and think about the kindest, most encouraging thing anyone ever said to you. Got it? My guess is it didn't take you very long. You can probably recall it word for word. That is because those words will forever be imprinted on your soul.

Self-help guru Dale Carnegie said, "Perhaps you will forget tomorrow the kind words you say today, but the recipient may cherish them for a lifetime." We get incredible mileage out of encouraging words. When someone pays us a compliment we often find ourselves walking on air for days. Encouraging words can fill our spirits to overflowing; not only blessing us, but those around us.

In addition to sweetening our souls, a regular dose of encouraging words has lasting health benefits. Those trained in psychology know this to be true. There are various modes of therapy today that integrate the use of words to heal. Therapists have harnessed the power of words to motivate, inspire, and activate healing energies in people. Our words connect with our memory systems and can trigger the release of either healing or destructive powers. Greek playwright Aeschylus once said, "Words are the physicians of a mind diseased."

Another verse in the book of Proverbs speaks to the health benefits of encouragement: "Anxiety in the heart of man causes depression, but a good word makes it glad" (Prov. 12:25, NKJV). Few things cause our hearts to be more anxious and our spirits more depressed than critical, condescending words, especially from people to whom we look up. Positive, uplifting words from those whose opinions we value can brighten our hearts and spirits. Mother Teresa once said, "Kind words can be short and easy to speak but their echoes are endless."

Another nun, by the name of Sister Helen Mrosla, tells this story of the impact of encouraging words:

> He was in the third grade class I taught at Saint Mary's School in Morris, Minnesota. All 34 of my students were dear to me, but Mark Eklund was one in a million. Very neat in appearance, he had that happy-to-be-alive attitude that made even his occasional mischievousness delightful.
>
> Mark also talked incessantly. I tried to remind him again and again that talking without permission was not acceptable. What impressed me so much, though, was the sincere response every time I had to correct him for misbehaving. "Thank you for correcting me, Sister!" I didn't know what

to make of it at first but before long I became accustomed to hearing it many times a day.

One morning my patience was growing thin when Mark talked once too often. I made a novice teacher's mistake. I looked at Mark and said, "If you say one more word, I am going to tape your mouth shut!"

It wasn't ten seconds later when Chuck blurted out, "Mark is talking again." I hadn't asked any of the students to help me watch Mark, but since I had stated the punishment in front of the class, I had to act on it.

I remember the scene as if it had occurred this morning. I walked to my desk, very deliberately opened the drawer and took out a roll of masking tape. Without saying a word, I proceeded to Mark's desk, tore off two pieces of tape and made a big X with them over his mouth. I then returned to the front of the room.

As I glanced at Mark to see how he was doing, he winked at me. That did it! I started laughing. The entire class cheered as I walked back to Mark's desk, removed the tape and shrugged my shoulders. His first words were, "Thank you for correcting me, Sister."

At the end of the year I was asked to teach junior high math. The years flew by, and before I knew it Mark was in my classroom again. He was more handsome than ever and just as polite. Since he had to listen carefully to my instruction in the "new math," he did not talk as much in the ninth grade.

One Friday things just didn't feel right. We had worked hard on a new concept all week, and I sensed that the students were growing frustrated with themselves—and edgy with one another. I had to stop this crankiness before it got out of hand. So I asked them to list the names of the other students in the room on two sheets of paper, leaving a space between each name. Then I told them to think of the nicest thing they could say about each of their classmates and write it down.

It took the remainder of the class period to finish the assignment, but as the students left the room, each one handed me their paper. Chuck smiled. Mark said, "Thank you for teaching me, Sister. Have a good weekend."

That Saturday, I wrote down the name of each student on a separate piece of paper, and I listed what everyone else had said about that individual. On Monday I gave each student his or her list. Some of them ran two pages. Before long, the entire class was smiling. "Really?" I heard whispered. "I never knew that meant anything to anyone!" "I didn't know others liked me so much!"

No one ever mentioned those papers in class again. I never knew if they discussed them after class or with their parents, but it didn't matter. The exercise had accomplished its purpose. The students were happy with themselves and one another again.

That group of students moved on. Several years later, after I had returned from a vacation, my parents met me at the airport. As we were driving home, Mother asked the usual questions about the trip: How the weather was, my experiences in general. There was a slight lull in the conversation. Mother gave Dad a sideways glance and simply said, "Dad?" My father cleared his throat. "The Eklunds called last night," he began.

"Really? I said. "I haven't heard from them for several years. I wonder how Mark is."

Dad responded quietly. "Mark was killed in Vietnam," he said. "The funeral is tomorrow, and his parents would like it if you could attend." To this day I can still point to the exact spot on I-494 where Dad told me about Mark.

I had never seen a serviceman in a military coffin before. Mark looked so handsome, so mature. All I could think at that moment was, Mark, I would give all the masking tape in the world if only you would talk to me.

The church was packed with Mark's friends. Chuck's sister sang "The Battle Hymn of the Republic." Why did it have to rain on the day of the funeral? It was difficult enough at the graveside. The pastor said the usual prayers and the bugler played taps. One-by-one those who loved Mark took a last walk by the coffin and sprinkled it with holy water.

I was the last one to bless the coffin. As I stood there, one of the soldiers who had acted as a pallbearer came up to me. "Were you Mark's math teacher?" he asked. I nodded as I continued to stare at the coffin. "Mark talked about you a lot," he said.

After the funeral most of Mark's former classmates headed to Chuck's farmhouse for lunch. Mark's mother and father were there, obviously waiting for me. "We want to show you something," his father said, taking a wallet out of his pocket. "They found this on Mark when he was killed. We thought you might recognize it."

Opening the billfold, he carefully removed two worn pieces of notebook paper that had obviously been taped, folded, and refolded many times. I knew without looking that the papers were the ones on which I had listed all the good things each of Mark's classmates had said about him. "Thank you so much for doing that," Mark's mother said. "As you can see, Mark treasured it."

Mark's classmates started to gather around us. Chuck smiled rather sheepishly and said, "I still have my list. It's in the top drawer of my desk at home." John's wife said, "John asked me to put his in our wedding album. "I have mine too," Marilyn said. "It's in my diary." Then Vicki, another classmate, reached into her pocketbook, took out her wallet and showed her worn and frazzled list to the group. "I carry this with me at all times," Vicki said without batting an eyelash. "I think we all saved our lists."

That's when I finally sat down and cried. I cried for Mark and for all his friends who would never see him again. [15]

A Rare Gift

Why is it that all those students kept those notes for years? It's because words of affirmation, especially from those who are important to us, never lose their power. Without giving it a second thought, we toss in the garbage test papers and science fair projects that we spent hours preparing for and working on. Yet, we tuck away for safekeeping and hang onto for years notes of encouragement that we've received from people whose opinions matter to us. Maybe we in our culture cling to words of affirmation because they are so rare.

Fathers have more power to influence their children—for good or bad—than anyone else on earth. Fathers who are attuned to their children's needs for encouragement and who readily respond to those needs bless their children with a valuable gift. It is a gift that truly keeps on giving.

> **Fathers have more power to influence their children—for good or bad—than anyone else on earth.**

"Your Father Loves You!"

In their first televised interview after the tragedy, Christian recording artist Steven Curtis Chapman and his wife, Mary Beth, shared the heartrending story of their daughter's death. Five-year-old Maria Sue was playing in the yard when she noticed her seventeen-year-old brother's car coming down the street. As Will pulled into the driveway, she excitedly ran to greet him and darted into the path of his car. He couldn't stop in time.

Their father heard the screams and ran out of the house. He picked up his daughter and put her in the car to take her to the hospital. As he was backing out of the driveway he glanced up and saw his son. Will was still standing in the driveway, utterly inconsolable. Sensing his son's utter helplessness and ill-founded guilt, Steven Curtis immediately lowered his window and yelled loud enough for the whole neighborhood to hear, "Will Franklin, your father loves you!"

Will Franklin was blessed to have heard those words from his father thousands of times before. But they were never more encouraging as on that day. Those words in that moving, emotionally amped context conveyed more love, compassion, and encouragement than any other time his father spoke them.

When we feel all alone, helpless and hopeless, standing in the midst of our pain and guilt and loss our Heavenly Father calls out our name and says, "I love you!" He longs to speak words of encouragement to His kids, especially in those dark days when we need them the most. If we are not hearing the encouraging words of our Heavenly Father we're not listening hard enough.

I have made it a habit to ask God to help me hear His words of affirmation to me. I can get discouraged pretty easily. So I regularly pray that God will send encouragement my way. I am astonished at the creative ways He answers that prayer.

Encouraged Through Nature

Often God speaks encouragement to me through nature. He has, indeed, crafted a wonder-full world. As my relationship with Him has grown I have realized the truth of Martin Luther's words: "God writes the Gospel not in the Bible alone, but also on trees, and in the flowers and clouds and stars." I read and see and hear Him more and more through His creation.

When I view the sun, especially when it first peers across the horizon in the morning, I am encouraged in knowing that my Heavenly Father is, Himself, light. The psalmist speaks of God wrapping Himself in light. I don't know much about physics, but I know that light and darkness cannot coexist. When God shines His light in my life, the darkness that sometimes hovers over my soul is dispelled. Each sunrise is God lifting the curtain on a new day; a preview to coming attractions.

For me, the sun's brilliance has also come to symbolize the fulfillment of the promise of Jesus that one day God's children will "shine like the sun in the kingdom of their Father!" (Matt. 13:43, NIV). Heaven's brightness will make Yuma seem like a cavern.

God uses the stars as props to encourage me to never stop believing. My family goes camping in central Indiana every summer. It amazes me how once we get away from the lights and smog of the city the night sky seems to come alive, glistening with more stars than I ever knew existed. I'm no astronomer. When I look at the stars I not only don't see hunters or bulls or flying horses, I'm suspicious of those who do. It is reasonable to suggest that such constellations were "discovered" by astronomers after 2 a.m.—when the bars closed. But I am impressed by God's galaxies, nonetheless. When I gaze at the vast array of stars I am reminded of the Old Testament story in which God told a doubting Abraham—a seventy-five-year-old codger with an infertility problem—that his descendants would one day outnumber the stars of the sky. Sometimes when I look up at a stellar spectacle I can picture God looking down on the panorama, high-fiving Abraham, and saying, *That's what I'm talkin' about!*

The wind reminds me of God because even though it is invisible, its effects are obvious. The Bible

A breeze across my face is God's whisper, *You're not alone. I'm here.*

tells us that wind is a symbol of God's Spirit coming upon His people, sent to comfort and convict us, to enable and encourage us, to train and teach us in the ways of God. A breeze across my face is God's whisper, *You're not alone. I'm here.*

Rain is a declaration that my Heavenly Father is my Provider. Every facet of my life, like every scene of the nature show, is under His divine direction. Rain is God's reminder that, whether I want to acknowledge it or not, I am completely dependent on Him and must look to Him continually to supply my needs. My wife's grandmother recalled a common scene from her youth. Most men in her church were farmers. Their livelihood was dependent on rainfall. She told how after the Sunday morning church service the first thing the men did when they stepped outside was to look at the sky. Not a bad practice.

Thunder is God's pronouncement to me that He is just plain awesome. I realize that *awesome* is an overused word in our culture, as is its frequent companion—*dude*. Both were finalists in a recent poll conducted by *The New Yorker* asking which word readers would like to see eliminated from the English language. But there is no more perfect adjective than *awesome* when describing the lightning-induced reverberation that rumbles across the heavens during an electrical storm. It is a sound that literally (another word on *The New Yorker* list) fills me with awe—a sense of reverence for and wonder of God. In Psalm 29, David uses the metaphor of thunder to describe how God's voice is powerful, majestic, and reverberating.

Bird watching has become a religious experience of sorts for me. I find pleasure in knowing that God is a bird watcher Himself. The Bible says that the Heavenly Father knows every bird; that He watches over them; that a sparrow can't even fall to the ground without Him knowing it. I haven't spotted too many eagles in my lifetime but the mere mention of the word brings to my mind Isaiah 40:31, one of the most encouraging and empowering passages in all of Scripture: "But those who trust in the LORD will find new strength.

They will soar high on wings like eagles. They will run and not grow weary. They will walk and not faint" (NLT).

We have a number of bird feeders in our backyard as well as a little pond that birds use to drink from and bathe in. On any given day, all the colors from the Crayola eight-pack are represented—blue jays, cardinals, yellow finch, hummingbirds, purple martins, wrens, black birds, and orioles all stopping by for some grub, or grubs, as the case may be.

My biggest challenge has been keeping the squirrels from eating the food I put out for the birds. After considering various squirrel prevention plans, and eliminating those that involved bullets, I chose to go the cheapest route (I told you I was Dutch). In my research I discovered that squirrels have taste buds but birds do not. An area nursery sold bottles of potent spices to mix with bird seed, a PETA-approved procedure I was assured would solve my squirrel situation. I bought a bottle and, just to ensure immediate and lasting results, I doubled the amount of spices I was to add to the seed. Little did I know, my squirrels love Mexican. My new plan is to feed them until they're too fat to climb up the poles.

God can even use rascally rodents to teach life lessons. Squirrels are God's reminder to me that even when I am annoyed by the behavior of others, we are all God's creatures.

Encouraged Through People

As we've already discovered in this chapter, God, in addition to nature, also uses people to pass along to us His words of encouragement. There have been times in my life when I've felt like I had a KICK ME sign on my back; times when difficulties and disappointments come one right after the other; times when I just want the world to stop so I can get off. Yet, it seems that at the moment I determine that I can't go on, God dispatches an unsuspecting soul to come into my life and give me what I need most at that very moment. I will get a phone call, a note, a text message, or even perhaps "randomly" bump into someone who is clearly an undercover agent of God sent to deliver His personal words of encouragement. Doubt calls these coincidences. I call them God-incidences, orchestrated by a Heavenly Father who knows precisely when my courage needs replenishing.

When I first went into full-time ministry my mentor encouraged me to keep a file of kind notes and cards I received. "Trust me, you'll need it," he said. I followed his advice. I can't tell you how many times when I've been down and discouraged that I've pulled out my Encouragement File and felt a hug of calming reassurance from my Heavenly Father through the thoughtful words of others.

Encouraged Through the Written Word

Another effective means of encouragement that God has used in my life is the written word; not just the Bible, but books, blogs, devotionals, and magazine articles that have helped guide me along on this expedition called life. It's astounding how many authors who don't know me have written books for or about me. God has often used the words of complete strangers to convey His personal message to me.

I had an aunt who used to say that my uncle didn't have a hearing problem he had a listening problem. God speaks words of encouragement to us all day long. Are you listening for them?

I used to be leery of people who say that God told them to do stuff. That was before God started telling me to do stuff. It was in a hotel conference room in a Chicago suburb in 2007 when God very clearly told me to write this book. Jan and I were at FamilyLife Marriage Retreat and, for this particular session, the men had been separated from the women. The speaker who addressed us guys began his talk with a question. He asked, "What is the first word that comes to your mind when you think of your father?" We were instructed to shout out our answers from wherever we were sitting. I was seated toward the back and watched with interest as several men shared. The first man to respond yelled out, "Supportive!" Another added, "Encouraging!" In quick succession I heard "Loving!" "Strong!" "Caring!" Then came the silence. Don't think that God doesn't speak in silence. After a few seconds He gave one of the men the courage to change the tone. "Absent," he shouted. Another pause. "Alcoholic," shared another. Then in rapid fire: "Angry." "Distant." "Mean." "Abusive."

The pain in the room was tangible. God confirmed in my heart right then and there that way too many people are carrying father wounds and that I needed to do something about it. When the wives returned to the room for the next session I greeted Jan with, "I'm going to write a book."

In the following weeks, even though God's directive was clear I was still kind of fuzzy about when this book writing venture was supposed to happen since I had just followed His leading to take a church staff position. I put the book project on the back burner, but God kept pulling it to the front.

For three years God nudged, prodded, and elbowed me. I was poked more than the Pillsbury Doughboy. I needed a time-out. I needed some time away with God—just the two of us—so I could be clear about how and when His plan would be implemented. I signed up to spend a week at a pastors' retreat center in Wisconsin. After all, listening for God is easier when there's nothing else of great interest going on.

I prayed all the way there. No baseball broadcasts. No talk radio. I didn't even sing with Darlene Zschech. I spent three hours on the toll road talking with God. I needed clarity but, apparently, I thought God needed it, too. I had already crossed the Wisconsin border when I found myself still trying to make clear to Him why maybe writing this book wasn't such a good idea.

My church job was very demanding. Jesus would have been hard-pressed to fill my job description. It was out of the question that this book would be written in my spare time. I had none. All indications were that if I was going to write this book I was going to have to resign from my church job. God needed to know that from both a family and financial perspective that was just a stupid thing to do. I needed an income. My family needed health insurance. My wife needed stability.

I didn't wait until I arrived at the retreat center to retreat. While still driving God's Spirit brought me to the place where I relented, "If you are calling me to quit my job and write a book I will do it, but I'm kind of dense so you're going to have to spell it out for me. Hit me upside the head with a two-by-four if you have to. Just make Your will clear."

After checking into my room and getting settled, I stretched out in the recliner in front of a window overlooking the lake and reached into my briefcase for the book I was just about finished reading. It was then I realized I had grabbed the wrong book. I growled and thought some words that I may have said out loud if there weren't other pastors around. I looked reluctantly at the book that I had brought —*Life of the Beloved* by Henri Nouwen. I had bought it sometime earlier but it was somewhere in the middle of my must read list.

Since it was the only book I had with me I started reading. In the introduction Nouwen wrote of an encounter with a reporter from the town in which Nouwen had a speaking engagement. It was obvious to Nouwen that the reporter was unsettled in his life so he asked, "If you could do anything in the world what would you do?"

The man said that he would write a book.

Nouwen's response: *So quit your job and write a book.*

I laughed out loud. Talk about a God-incidence. I ask God to make His will clear to me and He does so with words that couldn't be more direct, found in a book I had taken with me by "accident."

Our Heavenly Father is continually speaking words of encouragement to us.

The words, "Quit your job and write a book" were my two-by-four. They weren't just Henri Nouwen's words of encouragement to a reporter. They were God's encouraging words to me—now circled, underlined, and highlighted in my copy of Nouwen's book. Upon returning home from the retreat, I wrote my letter of resignation from church ministry, gave my financial needs to God, and began writing.

For added measure, as if "Quit your job and write a book" wasn't direct enough, God then sent me this message via a fortune cookie from my favorite Chinese restaurant: *You will become an accomplished writer.* Seriously? Who gets fortune cookie messages like that?

Words have power. Our Heavenly Father is continually speaking words of encouragement to us. His words at times lift our spirits. Other times they give us clarity. Sometimes they make us laugh out loud. If you can't hear them you're not listening hard enough.

CHAPTER 9

A Father Who Wants To Spend Time With Us

God wants to speak to us more than we want to listen.
He is a God of love, and love longs to communicate.

Linda Schubert

My dad never played catch with me. We never flew a kite or built a model car together. I have no recollections of his taking me to a ballgame or even taking the time to sit on the bed next to me to say goodnight, let alone read me a bedtime story. One would think that when he asked me to go ice fishing with him one Saturday morning in January, I would have been doing cartwheels. But even at age eight I could read between the lines better than an L.A. divorce attorney—a skill fine-tuned by observing the subversive interactions in a turbulent alcoholic environment.

My exuberance at the chance to spend some time with my dad was offset by my awareness that he was coerced. On more than one occasion during the previous week, when I was still in bed and my father was in the kitchen about to leave for work, I overheard my mother nagging him—known in Christian circles as "encouraging"—to do something with me. I believe her exact words were, "It wouldn't kill you to spend some time with your son."

So when the offer finally came, I was painfully aware that it was not exactly heartfelt. His invitation to take me ice fishing was not prompted so much by his desire to have his son by his side as to have his wife off his back. Nevertheless, I jumped at the opportunity.

It didn't matter that the temperature the day we went fishing was in the teens and that the wind blew directly in my face no matter which direction I was facing. It didn't matter that despite offering the juiciest of night crawlers there was no concrete evidence that fish actually existed beneath the eight inches of ice. It didn't matter that our father-son conversation was crippled by an inability to communicate in a meaningful manner. What mattered was that my dad and I were spending time together.

We sat next to each other on that frozen lake all morning—the most time we ever spent together, just the two of us. There was very little comradery. There was even less fishing since, by definition, fishing infers the presence of fish. After almost three hours of inactivity we declared the fish the winners, packed up our gear, and headed for home.

Or so I thought.

Sit Tight

The heater in his maroon 1962 Chevy pickup had barely begun to live up to its name when Dad pulled off the road in front of a laundromat. "Sit tight. I've got to run in here a minute," he said as he stepped out of the truck and slammed the door. I knew he had no clothes that needed washing. *Why did we stop here?*

I glanced across the street. As soon as I saw the red neon beer mug flickering in the window, my heart began to hurt. I watched my father disappear into Earl's Tap, an establishment I had overheard him reference many times in bull sessions with his buddies. It was one of his favorite watering holes.

Sitting tight was not a problem. With no seatbelt laws yet in existence I was already sitting on the edge of the front seat. The less contact my rear end made with the vinyl seat cover the better. One thing about vinyl. It is a startling conductor of cold.

Although boredom and sub-freezing temperatures are mutually exclusive, I began looking for ways to divert my mind from the intense conditions. Since my breath was clearly visible I managed to kill some time trying to make smokeless smoke rings. That grew increasingly difficult when my mouth became too cold to make an *o*.

I rested my head against the window praying to God and anyone else who might be listening for the door of the tavern to open and my dad to come out. As I whispered my plea over and over again I discovered that the warmth of my breath created a thin layer of frost on the glass. That provided several minutes of distraction as I wrote, drew pictures, and played tic-tac-toe on the icy window, even though the use of my right forefinger was hampered by a heavy, stiff glove and my uncontrollable shivering.

As the minutes passed with the swiftness of a stalled freight train, I wiggled my toes and pressed my hands against my ears to prevent them from freezing solid. Even as a third grader I knew something was very wrong with this picture. Today, there are laws against keeping *animals* in parked cars.

I occasionally hugged myself to keep warm. If anything, the feeling of being hugged warmed my heart. I kept wondering why my father would leave me out in

I occasionally hugged myself to keep warm. If anything, the feeling of being hugged warmed my heart.

the cold, however, a fear of how I might respond to his answer prevented me from asking the question. Even more painful than the bitter cold was the bitter truth, at least as I saw it as an eight year old: My dad would rather spend time with his drinking buddies than with me.

I don't know how long I was alone in that truck. I do know it was long enough for my dad to get drunk.

I remained on the edge of the front seat all the way home. This was partly because it brought me closer to the heat vent and partly because I needed to be prepared to bail out at any time in case Dad's chemically altered navigational skills found us homing in on a tree. Sitting in that position proved to be a harbinger of sorts. I've spent much of my life on the edge of my seat anticipating danger.

Looking back on that Saturday morning still gives me chills— not because I remember feeling so cold, but because I remember feeling so alone. It wasn't that I wanted my dad to spend time with me. I wanted my dad to *want* to spend time with me. I wanted to be an important part of his life. I wanted to know that I mattered.

> **It wasn't that I wanted my dad to spend time with me. I wanted my dad to *want* to spend time with me.**

Poverty

Mother Teresa, who was within touching distance of people whose lives were ravaged by the likes of famine, disease, and death, believed that an even greater human indignity is loneliness. "We think that poverty is only being hungry, naked, and homeless," she said. "The poverty of being unwanted, unloved, and uncared for is the greatest poverty." Maybe there are more children in today's world "suffering in poverty" than we think.

There is a song from my era that speaks to a whole generation of children mired in meaninglessness as a result of being unwanted, unloved, and uncared for by their own fathers. The song begins with one of the most memorable introductions in pop music history; a simple, yet hauntingly powerful bass line. The bass is joined by percussion, then strings. A lead guitar enters, followed by a trumpet, all enmeshed in a morbid prelude that lasts a full two minutes. The eerie melody grabs you by the collar and forces you to pay attention to the lyrics that are as unpleasant to hear as the song's minor key.

More than a memorable melody, The Temptations' number-one hit, "Papa Was a Rollin' Stone" was an indictment on a fatherless culture; it's sad story disturbingly familiar to a generation of children left alone by their daddies.

The greatest poverty, undeniably, occurs when kids are abandoned by the one commissioned by God Himself to love and provide for them. No child wants to remember their papa as a rolling stone. We need our fathers to be solid rocks.

The Greater Problem

Some may say that the most significant issue facing our culture today is joblessness. Others might suggest that it's drug abuse or crime. Still others may bring up violence or intolerance. But in most cases these are just *symptoms* of a greater problem: fatherlessness. We need **We need to acknowledge that the breakdown of the family is the greatest contributing factor in the breakdown of our society.** to acknowledge that the breakdown of the family is the greatest contributing factor in the breakdown of our society.

The erosion of the family in America through the years is startling. In the 1900s children were seen as a blessing. Today, many parents view them as a burden. A century ago, fathers were present and active in their children's lives. Today, an alarming percentage of dads are passive or absent completely. Maybe housewives wouldn't be so desperate if their husbands were at home fulfilling their family obligations.

If the majority of fathers in this country took their role seriously and provided the love, instruction, and encouragement their children need and deserve; if dads taught their kids the value of hard work, respecting others, and honoring themselves; the results wouldn't just trickle down, they would flow like Niagara Falls. Drug abuse would lose its appeal because teens wouldn't want to escape a reality brimming with the undying love and support of a father. The crime rate would plummet as children would follow not only their dad's instruction but his example of how to treat others. There would even be financial consequences if fathers played an active and positive role in their children's lives. Imagine how our economy would flourish if laziness, apathy, and a sense of entitlement would give way to helpfulness, assertiveness, and a sense of pride.

Imprisoned

It should come as no surprise that the percentage of people in prison who have father issues runs at about 100 percent. I recently heard the story of a Catholic nun who served as a chaplain in a men's prison. One day a prisoner asked her to buy him a Mother's Day card to send to his mom. She did and, as the prisoner walked back to his cell with the card, the other prisoners asked where he got it. Soon there was a long line of prisoners outside the nun's office, all waiting to ask her to buy a card for them to send to their moms.

> **It should come as no surprise that the percentage of people in prison who have father issues runs at about 100 percent.**

The chaplain called Hallmark Cards and explained what had happened. Hallmark graciously offered to send three cases of discontinued Mother's Day cards to the prison. Every card in those three boxes was mailed out of that prison, bearing an appreciative inmate's signature.

Noticing that Father's Day was approaching, the nun put in another call to Hallmark to ask if they would be so generous as to donate some Father's Day cards as well. Again, Hallmark shipped three cases of cards to the prison. Father's Day came and went. All three boxes remained unopened. Not one prisoner thought enough of his father to send him a card that cost nothing.

Leaving the Cocoon is a wonderful ministry based in Franklin, Tennessee, that reaches out to incarcerated females. A team of ladies provides one-on-one mentoring to inmates in the local prison and continues to spend regular time with them after their release. The mentors provide loving support and encouragement, the likes of which many of the prisoners have never experienced before. In many instances, the volunteer is the first person in the prisoner's life who has made her feel that she actually matters.

The mentors also aid in the shaping of the prisoners' spiritual lives. They introduce the ladies to a God who many of them had never met before—a God who forgives, a God who heals, a God who loves them just as they are.

According to Leaving the Cocoon Executive Director Vicki Harvey-Helgesen, while most of the ladies are open to God's sovereignty, redemption, and grace, there is one facet of the Christian life the ladies find impossible to embrace. She said that upon their release, while many of the women have established a steady habit of prayer and devotions and may even attend church regularly, "there [was] not one ex-offender I have encountered who could say that they have an *intimate* relationship with their Father in Heaven."

For the vast majority of the prison population the words *father* and *intimate* don't even belong in the same paragraph. Prisoners who come to faith may *revere* their Heavenly Father. They may *pray to* Him. They may *worship* Him. But for many, the thought of *intimacy with* Him makes them put their hands up and turn away.

It's not that they don't want to spend time with God. It's that they sincerely doubt God wants to spend time with them.

163

When our dads don't invest in our lives it becomes easy to believe that we don't matter. And if we don't matter to our earthly father it is logical to conclude that we don't matter to a Heavenly Father either.

One of the most gratifying days of my life was the Saturday I led a Finding Father's Love Retreat for the women involved in Leaving the Cocoon. We spent the day talking about the intimacy our Heavenly Father desires in our relationship with Him; that He yearns for a closeness with His kids, especially those who don't know what closeness with a father is like. Few things are as fulfilling to me as seeing people, for the first time, discover how much they matter to their Heavenly Father.

The Lord's Work

I was at a church service a few years ago where a missionary couple was introduced whose furlough was coming to a close. After three months in the United States, their family was returning to Russia and had been asked to say a few words about their work there. From my church experience the combination of a missionary and a microphone is rarely a good thing. My mind began to wander just out of habit. Somehow after their introduction I couldn't get the Beatles tune "Back in the USSR" out of my mind.

My ears perked up, however, when the missionary mentioned that not everyone in the family was returning to Russia. He explained that since they had been back to America, their fifteen-year-old daughter became seriously ill and had to be hospitalized. It appeared she had contracted some strange virus. Doctors weren't sure what it was so she was undergoing a battery of tests.

With an eerie aura of piety the missionary proclaimed that since God was clearly calling them back to the mission field, they were leaving their daughter behind. Many in the congregation nodded their heads as if to say, *Wow, is this man committed!* I was shaking my head thinking, *Wow, this man needs to be committed!*

I have no doubt that his decision to leave his daughter in the hospital while he took the rest of the family back to Russia was the result of some sort of spiritual prompting. I'm just not sure it was the Holy Spirit doing the nudging.

I couldn't help but put myself in that girl's hospital slippers. *What would I feel toward my father? What would I feel toward the people in Russia who Dad deemed more important than me? What would I feel toward a God who would call a father to leave the side of his daughter's hospital bed so he could share Jesus's love with others?*

Now the Beatles were singing a different tune in my head: *Help, I need somebody!*

A pastor from a well-known megachurch shared that of all the groups he has spoken to around the world, the toughest crowd he has ever faced was a class comprised of missionary kids. At the mere suggestion that God wants us to live lives that honor Him, these teens shut down faster than a keg at a Methodist potluck. For many of them, "honoring God" equated to yanking your kids out of their school, ripping them away from their friends, forcing them into a strange culture, then ignoring them so you could invest time in people who really matter to God.

As deplorable as it was growing up in an alcoholic home, I contend that, in many ways, it is more difficult to grow up with a dad who is addicted to work, particularly Christian work. I could blame my dad's lack of involvement in my life on his addiction to alcohol. Children of overcommitted clergy, ministry leaders, and missionaries are often neglected so their dads can minister to others who perhaps need the love of Jesus more than they do.

If these children were to ever confront their dad about not spending enough time with them, we can be sure the response would be some form of, *I'm doing the Lord's work.* That reply is so righteous it comes with an ironclad assurance of no follow-up questions. After all, it is one thing to question your father, it's quite another to question the Lord. Children of churchaholics are often left to conclude that the Lord's work involves fathers being in everyone's life but theirs. Papas don't have to be rolling stones to leave their kids feeling alone.

Black Sheep

Shari's self-portrait bore no resemblance to her picture-perfect father. If you were assembling a puzzle of a model Christian an image of Shari's dad would be on the box. More than just a parishioner, he was a pillar in the church. He was a perennial elder. He not only attended every weekend service, but meetings throughout the week as well. The few hours that he wasn't at church, he donated to the Gideons, placing Bibles in hotel rooms for sinners who stayed there.

There was no question that he was devout in his beliefs. But while Shari's dad was busy showing others the way, he didn't notice that Shari lost hers. She began smoking before she began driving. As a teen she was more familiar with alcoholic beverages than the average barkeep. Rappers would have found her language offensive. Shari's rebellion also propelled her into prostituting herself. It wasn't for the money. All boys needed to pay was attention.

While resenting it at first, Shari came to relish the label given her by her parents and their friends. She rather enjoyed being the black sheep. At least she was finally getting noticed. The people at church were talking more about Shari than they were about Jesus.

The people at church were talking more about Shari than they were about Jesus.

One day, a rather indignant elder from the church confronted her. He challenged her on her sinful behavior and wondered aloud what a disappointment she must be to her father. Seething, she shot back, "My father is so busy saving people's souls that he let me go to hell." Shari's response was found contemptible by the church folk. I found her words to be profoundly sad.

Every believer is called to do the Lord's work; namely, to seek and to save the lost. For those who are fathers, that work must begin at home.

A Father Who Pursues

The Heavenly Father does not deem some of his kids more worthy of His time than others. He desires a growing, thriving, loving relationship with each of His children—"red and yellow, black and white, all are precious in His sight."

The Bible is basically the story of a Father pursuing a relationship with His children. Take a moment to consider that word: *pursue.* It means *to follow; to chase; to hunt; to strive for.* We don't pursue something we merely have a mild interest in. We only pursue things that really matter. Now let me say it again: The Heavenly Father *pursues* a relationship with His children.

Some of us still blow that statement off faster than a campaign promise. That is an unfortunate result of either what we choose to believe about ourselves or what we choose to believe about God. Again, it's about choices.

Tobey Maguire's character in the film *Spiderman 3* offered these words of wisdom: "Whatever comes our way, whatever battle we have raging inside us, we always have a choice. It's the choices that make us who we are."

Perhaps a more credible source of wisdom is Scottish minister and teacher J. Oswald Chambers who once said, "We are at this moment as close to God as we really choose to be."

Choosing to believe that our Heavenly Father pursues us is also choosing to believe that we

> **Choosing to believe that our Heavenly Father pursues us is also choosing to believe that we are worth being pursued.**

are worth being pursued; that God not only follows us, He chases after us. He isn't just lukewarm about the idea of a close relationship with us, He strives for intimacy with us. Why? *Because we matter.*

A familiar Christian phrase is "spending time with God." That could mean a number of things: praying to Him, attending church services, meditating on His Word, reading devotionals, listening to Christian music. Each of these activities can bring us into closer relationship with God. But in each of these activities *we* are the pursuers.

It is when we understand that God pursues *us* that our relationship reaches lofty levels. For some, the thought of a father wanting to spend time with His children is incomprehensible. Our father experience may have been such that we are left to believe that we aren't all that important. When our dads don't invest in our lives, it becomes easy to believe that we don't matter. And if we don't matter to our earthly father, we may well ask why we would matter to a Heavenly Father. Seeing ourselves as undesirable builds a wall between us and the Father—every feeling of rejection, every twinge of unworthiness is a cinderblock cemented by hopelessness.

An Unbreakable Bond

Jesus's story of the prodigal son, which is found in Luke 15 and was referenced earlier in this book, is a powerful parable of the unbreakable bond between a father and his child; a bond infinitely stronger than the son's shame. Among the many lessons to be learned from this fascinating story is that the love of the Heavenly Father is so strong it can blast through any self-built walls of inadequacy.

Make no mistake about it. The son in Jesus's story had reason to feel guilty. He had thumbed his nose at his father, thumbed through his wad of ill-gotten inheritance cash, then thumbed a ride out of town. Even though he was not entitled to it, he asked for his father's inheritance overlooking one small detail—his father was still alive. In essence, by requesting the funds before the funeral, he was wishing his father dead. Though he didn't have to, his father gave him the money. The son then went off to a distant country and proceeded to squander it all on a variety of activities, none of which would have received the Moral Majority's seal of approval.

The son soon found himself so destitute he was eating pig slop to survive. All that was left for him to swallow was his pride. He gulped hard and headed back home.

What do you think might be going on in his mind as he made that journey? I imagine a conversation with himself that went something like this:

The closer I get the tighter my stomach feels. I'll never forget that look on his face when I asked him for the money. The hurt I saw in his eyes…

And why wouldn't he be hurt? I traded my family for a few nights out on the town. And what am I left with? No money, no food, no home, no family, no self-respect…

He won't even have to take me back into his house. I could live with the hired help.

But there's no reason on earth he should even do that. I am so ashamed. I guess all I can do is plead for mercy.

Meanwhile, back at the ranch, we would expect to find a father whose initial feelings of heartache, disappointment, and humiliation may have settled, but who was left with an anger toward his son that would smolder, if not blaze, for the rest of his life. But that is not the father this son came home to. Jesus told of the homecoming this way: "But while he was still a long way off, his father saw him and was filled with compassion for him; he ran to his son, threw his arms around him and kissed him" (Luke 15:20b, NIV).

Making this encounter even more unimaginable is that at this point *the son had not even apologized* to his dad. Lord knows, he had plenty of time in the pigpen to rehearse his "I'm sorry" speech, but before he could open his mouth he found himself on the receiving end of a hug that left him both drained and filled him at the same time.

As sinful humans this kind of love is hard for us to grasp. A cold shoulder from this father seems more appropriate than open arms. Imposing a long period of groveling would have made more sense. The father would have been justified in wanting to see to it that his son felt as much hurt as the boy caused him. This should have been the first recorded incident in Scripture of a parent uttering those immortal words, "I told you so." At the very least the father should have withheld any signs of affection until his son not only said "I'm sorry" but proved the depth of his remorse. These would have been more natural responses.

After all he had done, if I were the son and saw my father hike up his robe and start running toward me I would have hightailed in the opposite direction certain he had a weapon. Yet this father was only armed with hugs and kisses.

It is no secret that the father in Jesus's parable represents our Heavenly Father. The story is a touching, yet shocking portrayal of God's love and grace for His kids. It clearly conveys that there is no amount of heartache or disappointment that could possibly get in the way of our Heavenly Father's undying, unconditional, unmistakable love for us.

Despite our sinfulness, regardless of how many times we walk away from Him, our Heavenly Father can't wait for us to come back. He misses us when we're gone. He will always greet us with open arms when we again move in His direction. His relentless pursuit of us means one thing: We matter.

His relentless pursuit of us means one thing: we matter.

The Bible tells us that "while we were yet sinners Christ died for us" (Rom. 5:8, NIV). God values His children so much that He paid the ultimate price for us. He allowed His Son, Jesus, to die so that we might have life. What's more, He didn't wait until we first achieved a required level of holiness. He didn't withhold His blessing from us until we met a certain set of standards. He paid the greatest price for us *while we were yet sinners.* All because of His overwhelming desire to have us by His side.

Delighted

When it comes to His kids God doesn't just love us, He *delights* in us.

Here's a great bedtime verse that is much less terrifying than the one I was taught as a child about "dying before I wake": "For the LORD your God is living among you. He is a mighty savior. He will take delight in you with gladness. With his love, he will calm all your fears. He will rejoice over you with joyful songs" (Zeph. 3:17, NLT). Our Heavenly Father delights in us!

As a married parent of three children, two of which are girls, my son and I were in the minority whenever there was a vote on family activities. As a result, we watched more romantic comedies at the theater than any male should have to endure. Our youngest, Traci, is still captivated by mushy movies. She doesn't just observe the characters played by Julia Roberts or Kate Hudson or Jennifer Lopez as they predictably leave the person they're engaged to in their quest for deeper love, she *becomes* them. She feels what they feel.

As Traci entered her teen years, there were times I would offer to take her to see the latest romantic comedy, just the two of us. Not because romcoms had begun to grow on me. I would still have preferred to watch *The Three Stooges*. Or a baseball game. Or eye surgery. But I didn't take my daughter to the theater to watch the movie. I went to watch her.

As a father, I delighted in seeing my daughter enjoy herself. Whenever there was a tender moment in the movie, I would sneak a peek at her. Seeing that smile when the lead characters finally kissed was worth the $20 admission price and the $49 I paid for the popcorn and two medium sodas.

Our Heavenly Father delights in us. Even though He has a universe to run, He often takes His eyes off the big screen so He can watch His children respond to life's pleasures, whether it be a long-awaited smooch, a triple fudge brownie, a game-winning touch-down, or a majestic sunset. Our smiles make Him smile.

In the Presence

Spending time with God is a non-negotiable part of my life. Most times it happens outside of church. It often doesn't involve Bible reading, music, or meditation. It is not about *doing* anything. It is about *being* in the presence of a Heavenly Father who wants to spend time with me.

Let the record show this did not come naturally for me. Being Dutch, I am genetically predisposed to being a hard worker. Being a child of an alcoholic, perfectionism and people-pleasing are deeply ingrained in me. Learning how to stop *doing* and simply *be* necessitated a period of adjustment.

Several years ago when our kids were young, Jan and I took them to Disney World. Once we booked the trip some friends from church lent us a published guide on how to *do* Disney. It outlined a detailed strategy on how to squeeze every drop of pleasure out of the Disney experience. Based on data that considered traffic patterns, human behavior, the time of day, the popularity of the attractions, even the weather, the book suggested what rides to go on first, what shortcuts could be taken to get to them faster, even which lines moved quicker. (In case you're wondering, the line on the left is generally shortest because most people are right-handed and gravitate toward the right. The only exception is when I am in the line on the left. Then you will surely want to be in the other line.)

Another thing about the Dutch—we're frugal. It is said that copper wire first came into existence when two Dutchmen were fighting over a penny. We're all about getting the most for our money. Considering a Disney vacation for a family of five costs roughly the same as tuition for one year at Harvard, it was imperative that the strategies outlined in the Disney guide be implemented fastidiously. I guarantee you that when our family stepped off the tram at the Magic Kingdom, I had each subsequent step mapped out so we wouldn't waste a second.

It didn't take long to discover that the bigger waste of time was reading that book. As soon as I hustled my wife and kids through the gate—in the line farthest to left—and led the charge to Space Mountain, which statistically has the shortest lines when the park first opens, something happened that defied the well researched data. As I was frenetically pulling my kids into my agenda, they looked up and saw— in Technicolor—the cast of Toy Story. "Woody! Buzz!" they screamed as they yanked themselves free of my determined grasp and latched onto the larger-than-life characters.

What the "how to do Disney" book and this father who studied it didn't take into consideration was that my children were not nearly as interested in *doing* the rides and attractions as they were in just *being* in the presence of their beloved cartoon characters.

Be Still

Sadly, for many believers the Christian life is all about religious activity. We plot, we plan, we rush from one meeting or activity to the next, dragging our kids along, always going to the line on the left, as we try to cram as many activities into each day as possible before falling into bed at night totally exhausted. The Devil deceives us into thinking that all this activity has brought us closer to God. John Ortberg once said, "if the Devil can't make you bad he'll make you busy." Smart fella, that Ortberg.

Our Heavenly Father has a different strategy to help us draw closer to Him. He simply says, "Be still and know that I am God" (Ps. 46:10, NIV). Not *get busy,* but *be still. Stop what you're doing. Put away the to-do list. Dispose of all distractions. Silence your electronic devices. Just. Be. Still.*

I remember being in a church leadership meeting where the pastor had just come back from a spiritual retreat in which he had a sweet time of practicing the presence of God. Still glowing from the experience he asked the leaders, "When was the last time you got alone with God where you weren't reading the Bible or even praying, but were just spending time with the Heavenly Father?"

The sound of crickets gave them away. There wasn't a *first* time they had done that. It's not that they weren't good people. They were dedicated to serving God. They were hard workers in the church. But while they were active in *doing* things for their Heavenly Father they were alarmingly passive in terms of simply *being* with Him.

It is in solitude that our Father in Heaven speaks most clearly.

While God Himself said *it is not good for man to be alone* (Gen. 2:18), it is key to our mental and spiritual health to get away from others from time to time to seek solitude. I am not advocating running away from life. I am advocating running to God. It is in solitude that our Father in Heaven speaks most clearly.

Many people today are frightened by stillness. One reason is that we have grown accustomed to being in busy, noisy environments. We are bombarded daily by extraneous words and noises from our iPads and iPods, our Bluetooths and Blu-Rays, our PCs and MP3s. Sometimes we even hear sounds emanating from real people. When we surround ourselves with constant noise, the sound of silence can be scary.

While some are frightened of stillness *even if* God is there, others are frightened of it *because* God is there. The thought of being alone with God can bring back memories of times we were alone with our father. The very idea of being in the presence of the Heavenly Father can cause our face to flush and palms to sweat. Rather than put ourselves in an environment that might unsettle long buried feelings of fear, sadness, anger, betrayal, or rejection, we choose to avoid stillness at all costs. We medicate ourselves with activity. And our Heavenly Father weeps.

He misses us when we're away—even when we're off doing "His" work. He longs to spend time with us. He wants to know about our day. He cares about what we're thinking—what makes us cry and what makes us laugh. He delights in just being near us.

A Revelation

Something that has greatly enhanced my time alone with the Heavenly Father is a revelation I had about prayer.

> **My prayers were so exhaustive that God couldn't have gotten a word in edgewise.**

For much of my Christian life, my prayers consisted of praising, confessing, pleading, and thanking. So basically I was doing all the talking. But prayer, by definition, is *communication with God*. Not *to* Him. *With* Him. The Latin root of the word *communication* is *communis*, which means *to share*. I discovered that even though I was a Christian adult, I was a spiritual toddler. I had to learn how to share. My prayers were so exhaustive that God couldn't have gotten a word in edgewise.

So, one day, when I ran out of things to talk about, I decided to give God the floor. That decision proved to be the energy drink to my spiritual exercise routine. Now, many times when I pray, I pray "God to Dan" instead of "Dan to God." I pray as if my Heavenly Father was speaking to me, basing the dialogue on biblical facts that I know to be true. Listening for His voice has made our time together even more special. Henri Nouwen once said, "The real work of prayer is to become silent and listen to the voice that says good things about me."

Do you struggle to believe that God is a Father who delights in you, who wants to spend time with you? If so, I urge you to carve out some time alone with Him soon, time to do nothing but listen to what He has to say to you. You may want to use the "God to you" prayer that follows as a guide. What would your loving Father call you? Think about the person you feel closest to. When your best friend addresses you, what name or nickname does he or she use? Write that name in the blank at the beginning of the prayer. As you slowly and thoughtfully read through the prayer, picture the Heavenly Father looking into your eyes, a welcoming smile on His face. He's been waiting to spend this time with you. He wants to share with you how much you mean to Him. Wallow in His words.

> *Oh, _____, it is so good to be with you. You don't know how I miss you when you're gone.*
>
> *I know that making yourself vulnerable by coming to me like this is hard for you. I know how you've been hurt. I know that trust does not come easy once it's been betrayed. I know how you've been wounded by people close to you. In fact, I know everything about you. It's time you know everything about me.*
>
> *I am a perfect father. I am perfect in all my ways. I love you with a perfect love. I offer my children perfect peace.*
>
> *My love for you is everlasting. Nothing you could ever do will jeopardize it. My love for you is without condition. There is nothing you could do to make me love you more. There is nothing you could do to make me love you less.*
>
> *How I long for you to fully experience that love! I see how afraid you are. You're afraid of not measuring up. You're afraid of being rejected. You're afraid you will never find the peace you're looking for. And you're not alone. Since the creation of the earth my children have feared those same things. But I offer a solution. There is one thing that will cast fear out of your life—perfect love.*
>
> *When you know my love, when you experience it in the depths of your soul, it will become clear that you have nothing to be afraid of.*

I love you so much that at the very beginning of time I chose you to be my child. I formed you in your mother's womb. I gave life to you. I have claimed you as my own. I treasure you. I delight in you. You make me dance with joy.

I know why you have certain misunderstandings about Me. But please hear what I'm about to say. I am not angry; I am the complete expression of love. I am not distant; I am always with you. I will never go back on my word; I can be trusted. I know that you have experienced the pain of betrayal but know this: I have never broken a promise to my kids.

I am aware that there are things that happen in your life that you don't understand. I know that at times you have more questions than answers. I know that sometimes life doesn't make sense. Could I ask you something? Will you trust me anyway? Will you hold onto me knowing that I have your best interests in mind?

You may never get answers to your questions on this earth. But one day, when your faith in me through Jesus my Son becomes sight and we are together in heaven, I will show you the book of your life. You will then see how I carefully weaved together every incident, every word, every joy, every hurt to create a story with the happiest of endings—you and me, together forever, in a world that knows no tears, no fears, no death, no desertion, no failures, no fatherlessness.

And remember this, my child—My lap is always open. I look forward to spending time with you. I hope to have a lot more of it. That's because I love you. Not because of anything you've done. But because of who you are. You. Are. Mine.

What a thought—we have a Father who wants nothing more than to spend time with us. A Father who wouldn't think of leaving us alone. A Father who will never leave us out in the cold.

CHAPTER 10

A Father Who Is Pleased With Us

A father's disappointment can be a very powerful tool.

Michael Bergin, Actor

Every December the mailbox across the street with our house numbers on it produces some of the greatest works of fiction ever composed. They are written by family and friends from all around the country. They are commonly known as the annual Christmas letter. Reading these fabled family updates is the equivalent of being licked on the face by a litter of slobbering puppies.

Dear Loved Ones,

Another year has come and gone, and what a wonderful year it was! As many of you are aware, on Valentine's Day we were blessed with a new addition to our family! After a rather intense ten minutes of labor our bright and beautiful bundle of joy, Sara Sue, made her arrival. Her ready smile, not to mention a full head of curly hair, made everyone in the delivery room melt! We were delighted when Sara Sue took her first step at three months—although according to her grandmother, this was two weeks later than her father began walking!

Steve, after a successful ten-year career in the software business, is set to retire in May! In addition to working on his golf game, he plans on spending some time sprucing up the landscaping at our winter home in Palm Springs! I'm so glad we decided to buy condos instead of houses in Aruba and Jamaica—they are much less work!

As for me, I'm enjoying being a stay-at-home mom! I'm also actively involved in my charity work! You know me—always willing to lend a helping hand to those less fortunate!

We'd love to see you during the holidays but next week we're off to Aspen for our biannual ski trip! I already bought Sara Sue her first little pair of skis!

Anyway, we hope you have a wonderful Christmas season filled with God's richest blessings!

Love always,
The Smiths

Did I mention I can't stand puppies licking my face? I propose a new postal regulation that all Christmas letters come equipped with barf bags. Thankfully, God has blessed me with the gift of discernment. When reading these years-in-review I have deduced that if there are more exclamation points than periods at the end of sentences the content is more than likely as fake as a Chicago Cubs World Series ring.

While I readily dismiss most Christmas letters as sheer hyperbole, there is one family update we received years ago that my mind refuses to relinquish. In it a mother gave a saccharine sweet synopsis of the lives of her three eldest children, but then came the unexpected twist. She concluded her report by launching into a disturbing diatribe about her "rebellious" youngest child. Amber's parents publicly announced via the annual Christmas letter that their daughter was not following their set program for her life. It seems Amber was "wasting her time" with music and acting. She didn't want to pursue the career or attend the college her parents had chosen for her, but instead was performing in theatrical productions in school and in the community, as well as playing lead guitar in a local band. Amber's parents felt strangely obliged to let family and friends know that their youngest was "making poor choices" and "not living up to her potential." As if those comments didn't cause Amber enough embarrassment, the letter of holiday cheer concluded with five words which I can only hope her parents will one day find regrettable: *Amber is such a disappointment.*

Knowing the family as I do, had Amber been allowed rebuttal time the truth would have been revealed: The problem was not so much Amber as her parents. For her entire life Amber fell short of her mother and father's expectations. From the time she could walk and talk she clearly didn't fit their mold. When her father saw her coloring as a child, holding the crayon in her left hand, he insisted she was using the "wrong hand." When she was old enough to eat at the kitchen table and began holding her fork in her left hand her father used an extension cord to tie her left hand behind her back to teach her the "normal" way of doing things.

Amber was cut from a different cloth than her father. She was a free spirit. Her father operated by the book. Amber's life philosophy was "if it's not broken, break it." Her father had a death grip on status quo. Amber was spontaneous. Her father enforced regimen.

> **Even children of physically abusive parents will tell you that they would rather their parents were angry with them than disappointed in them.**

Rather than delight in their daughter's individuality, Amber's parents were displeased that she was different. They were not just disappointed with the things she did. They were disappointed with her.

A Parent's Disappointment

Feeling like you can never please your parents can be a curse. Even children of physically abusive parents will tell you that they would rather their parents were angry with them than disappointed in them.

An enlightening documentary on the life of *Tonight Show* host Johnny Carson revealed how this seemingly successful, satisfied, self-assured entertainer was desperate for the approval of his parents, his mother in particular. According to Carson's friend, Carl Reiner, Johnny "couldn't get a compliment out of his mother." She had expressed disappointment in his career choice. She was quite sure he would never make it in show business and was unwilling to acknowledge the fact that he did. When he once called her to share the news that he had been chosen the winner of the prestigious Governor's Award for his body of work in the television industry, her only response was, "I guess they know what they're doing."

Biographer Bill Zehme said that Johnny sought his mother's love and approval "until the day she died." Doc Severinsen, the *Tonight Show* band leader, shared that when Johnny's mother died a box was found in her house containing decades' worth of newspaper and magazine clippings about her famous son. Carson kept that box in his bedroom closet for the rest of his life. All it might have taken for Johnny Carson to experience the peace and contentment he spent his lifetime searching for was a simple, *I'm proud of you, son.*

Troublesome Traits

In 1983, therapist and author Dr. Janet G. Woititz developed a list of characteristics of adults who grew up in alcoholic homes.[16] These traits are also common in the lives of those who grew up feeling that they are a disappointment, whether their parents drink or not.

We judge ourselves without mercy. A child's logic simply says, "Dad is not pleased with me. I am a disappointment." This thinking carries into our adult life. We beat ourselves up for displeasing others—particularly our parents. We take full blame for their discontent. We don't just see ourselves as having *caused* disappointment. We believe we *are* a disappointment.

Derek so impressed his P.E. teacher with his wrestling skills that he was encouraged to try out for the high school wrestling team. Derek received accolades from fellow wrestlers, his coach, coaches from opposing teams, friends, and classmates—just about everyone except the ones he needed affirmation from the most: his parents. Derek's father, in particular, saw his son's activity as "a colossal waste of time."

Derek's dominance on the mat earned him a spot on the varsity team as a sophomore, which was unheard of in that high school conference. He had the makings of an all-state wrestler and was in line for a full-ride college scholarship when the unthinkable happened. While pinning yet another opponent Derek felt a pop in his knee. Knee ligament strains and tears are common in the world of wrestling and are very treatable. However, Derek's father saw this as an opportunity to teach him a lesson. He would not allow his wife to take Derek to the doctor. By refusing medical care for his son, Derek's dad finally got his way. Derek would never "waste his time" wrestling again.

Now in his late-twenties, Derek still walks with a limp. Every twinge of pain is accompanied by a tinge of shame, a constant reminder that there is a price to pay for displeasing your parents.

We guess at what normal is. I met Andy several years ago. Andy's dad was in prison for dealing drugs. Andy was an only child who lived with his mother. Mom was a drug addict by day and a prostitute by night. Andy shared with me that when he got up for school his mom was fast asleep after working all night. Andy would make his own breakfast, pack himself a lunch, and get himself off to school.

After school, Mom would still be sleeping off the drugs. There were weeks they never spoke to each other. While other kids in his class only had to do a little homework before going to bed at night, Andy's after school to-do list was extensive. He had to take over many of his parents' responsibilities. He cleaned the house, at least he cleaned it as best he could without being able to run the vacuum cleaner for fear of waking his mother. He shopped for groceries with money he would find in his mom's purse. He cooked supper for himself, but also prepared enough for his mom to have something to eat when she got up. Andy would take extra money he found around the house and bring it to the bank on Saturday mornings and make a deposit. He had taken charge of the checkbook to make sure the rent and utilities were paid.

One more thing I should mention. When Andy first told me his story he was ten years old. It took every ounce of my strength for me not to weep in front of him.

Andy's norm was that fathers don't live at home, that mothers need to do whatever it takes to survive, and that ten-year-old kids buy groceries and balance checkbooks. While this was Andy's norm he was pretty sure it wasn't normal. But he had no idea what normal was. This confusion about what is and isn't normal doesn't clear up when children grow up and move out of the house. Children from dysfunctional home environments become adults who are prone to question whether their own thoughts, feelings, and actions, as well as those of others, are to be considered normal.

We often have difficulty in following a project through from beginning to end. Nothing can snuff out a child's conscientious spirit quicker than a parent's constant criticism. Children who know they will be criticized no matter what they do can soon develop a "why bother?" attitude.

> **Nothing can snuff out a child's conscientious spirit quicker than a parent's constant criticism.**

When I was a boy, once my chin cleared the handle of our lawnmower, I was responsible for cutting the grass. But had I trimmed each blade on my hands and knees with manicure scissors and a ruler, I knew even before I yanked the pull cord that the job I did wouldn't be good enough for my father. Being an alcoholic dictates that you must regularly point out shortcomings in others so that no blame falls on you. *You didn't set the blade low enough. You didn't get close enough to the rocks. You have to rake when you're done mowing if you're going to let the grass get that tall.*

When I was a child, I talked like a child, I thought like a child, I reasoned like a child. And I believed that if I would just get it right I would one day meet my father's approval. I remember once mowing the lawn before my dad even told me to do it. Surely that would prove that I was a good kid; that would make Dad pleased.

I anxiously awaited his coming home from work. After he stumbled in to the kitchen, put his lunch box on the table, and tipped backward into the chair to take off his work shoes, he started railing on me for not being responsible enough to mow the lawn without having to be told. Before I could say a word my mother jumped to my defense. With hands on her hips for emphasis she said, "For your information, he mowed the lawn today."

Since admitting that he was too drunk to notice might suggest he could have a problem, he smugly responded, "Well he must have done a piss poor job if I can't even tell."

I struggle with finishing projects to this day. I continue to equate the completion of tasks—even the task of writing this book—as a public announcement that I am now open to judgment and criticism. Saying "I'm not finished with it yet" keeps fault finders at bay.

We have difficulty having fun. For no other reason than self-protection, children living in dysfunctional environments often seem to keep their guard up. We grow up to become adults who can relate to comedian Steven Wright who divulges, "You know how it feels when you're leaning back on a chair, and you lean too far back, and you almost fall over backwards, but then you catch yourself at the last second? I feel like that all the time." Because our antennas are always up to detect impending danger it becomes difficult, if not impossible, to let loose and have a good time.

It's no secret that many people who are therapists and counselors also see therapists and counselors because of their own issues.

Many of them struggle to follow in their own lives the advice they are quick to give to their clients.

A friend of mine once attended a national conference at a hotel for therapists and social workers which was held by a mental health organization. One of the organization's objectives was that each of the professionals in attendance address their own dysfunction to better equip them to help clients address their issues. The host agency set up a carousel in the lobby. All participants, many of whom who, despite their professional status, still struggled with having fun in their own lives, were required to ride the horsies. Brilliant.

We take ourselves very seriously. Our father's or mother's minimization of our feelings or accomplishments often sets us on a course to prove to ourselves and everyone else that we are important. Our primary objective in life becomes the building and preserving of our reputation. We obsess over what other people think about us. We become defensive when others challenge our thinking or question our motives. We cannot tolerate being teased. Being the butt of someone's joke is an affront to our very being. To us, constructive criticism is an oxymoron. Critical words, in any form, burn like acid.

William had a father who felt it was his duty to point out any imperfections he saw in his son. There was never a task William completed that fully met his father's approval. Even on the rare occasion that William's dad doled out a compliment to his son, a "but" was sure to follow. William's personal mission in life was to perform well enough to not hear that word ever again.

Today, William is a stand-up comedian. Although his job is to make people laugh, laughter is strangely absent in his off-stage life. After each performance William stands in the lobby soliciting feedback from audience members. Even if 99 percent of those polled said it was the greatest show on earth, William would come away feeling like a failure if just one person was the least bit critical. Though William has made a living by being funny, he has found people-pleasing to be serious business.

We have difficulty with intimate relationships. Marcy was six years old when her father told her mother that he had come to the realization that their marriage was a mistake. Apparently, he wasn't "cut out" to be a husband and father. So he gathered up his things and walked out the door. He sent his daughter token birthday cards for a couple of years, then all communication ceased.

Marcy's life was inalterably changed. In her teen years her quest for intimacy led her to open doors that were better left shut. Her love life resembled a merry-go-round with more boys getting on and off than she could even count. She had an unappeasable craving to experience the warmth and tenderness that would come from being close to a male who loved her. But she was operating under the false premise that sex equals love. While her date book was full, Marcy's life was unfulfilled.

Michelle grew up in a similar environment yet came to a very different conclusion about intimacy. She was bound and determined not to let anyone get close to her. To Michelle, allowing yourself to be intimate with someone only led to pain. Considered a knockout by any man with good eyesight, Michelle dated often. More than a handful of guys fell hard for her. But Michelle's fear of rejection overrode any possibilities of a serious relationship. She never had to concern herself with safe sex. She protected herself by rejecting others before they had the opportunity to reject her.

If it is indeed true that the fear of rejection has its roots in feeling like a disappointment to the people we care about the most, Marcy and Michelle are exhibits A and B. Likewise, many adult children of alcoholic or addicted fathers especially, are unfamiliar with the word *intimacy*. They will either go to great lengths to find it or go to great lengths to avoid it.

We constantly seek approval and affirmation. Something every person on the planet has in common is the need to love and be loved. That stands to reason since the Bible tells us that: (a) God is love, and that (b) we are made in His image.

It is perfectly natural to want approval and affirmation from others. However, when we experience disapproval from our parents a sometimes not so subtle shift takes place. We move from *wanting* the approval and affirmation of others to *needing* it.

People-pleasing is a full-time job with no benefits. Children who are products of healthy, functional environments are likely to become adults who are grateful to receive the approval and affirmation of others but not devastated when they don't. However, those from unhealthy family systems, who did not experience the approval and affirmation of a parent often go through life giving far more credence to the opinions of others than our own. In many cases, our self-worth is *dependent* on the affirmation and approval of others. People-pleasing is a full-time job with no benefits.

Rob was an honor roll student, chairman of the Key Club, and president of his high school class, yet couldn't seem to capture his father's attention. It was as if Rob was daily pumping quarters into a vending machine but every time walking away empty handed.

Rob's dad had been involved in denominational church leadership for some twenty years, a job that sent him to many parts of the world, but had effectively taken him out of Rob's world. Rob had just begun his senior year when his father informed him via e-mail that he had taken a position with a church plant in Nigeria. He and Rob's mother would be selling the house and moving immediately. He explained that he thought it best that Rob continue his education in the States. He made plans for Rob to live with a church family for the rest of the school year. Rob would then work for the summer before going on to college to pursue his dream of becoming a chemical engineer.

When Rob visited the college to chart out his course of study he dropped a bombshell on his guidance counselor. He had changed his mind about engineering. He declared that God had told him to seek a master of divinity degree. His new plan was to become a church planter for his denomination.

It took almost two decades for Rob to admit that it was a mistake. He found himself going through the motions in a job he wasn't gifted to do, involved in work he had no passion for. After several rounds of therapy prompted by the death of his father, Rob came to confess that his career choice wasn't so much driven by what God had said to him as by what his dad didn't say. Rob's father passed away without ever giving him the affirmation and approval he so desperately needed.

We are extremely loyal, even in the face of evidence that loyalty is undeserved. Children who have been brought up by parents who constantly voiced disapproval of them tend to develop a rather uncanny loyalty toward them. This misplaced allegiance is the result of children holding themselves responsible for their parents' continual state of disappointment. Even in cases where parents exhibit critical, even hurtful behavior, it is not uncommon for their children to remain earnestly loyal.

Beginning when she was just a little girl and continuing until she left home to attend college, Monique's father subjected her to unspeakable acts of violent, downright satanic deviance. Yet the thought of not having a father in her life was more terrifying than the devilish abuse he subjected her to. She believed that if she could just learn how to please him properly, she would be more deserving of his love and he wouldn't have to punish her anymore.

Monique, now married, continues to fetch her father's slippers and a fresh beer whenever she comes to visit. Monique has changed addresses but not circumstances. She often wears oversized sunglasses to hide her purple bruises and red eyes. The beatings from her husband are getting more frequent. But she will never leave him.

In the touching movie, *The Perks of Being a Wallflower*, a teenaged boy whose sister was being physically abused by her boyfriend asked his teacher why people choose to stay in relationships that are clearly not good for them. The instructor's ingenuous response: "We accept the love we think we deserve."

A Disappointment to God

There is an unfortunate spiritual component to years of being subjected to a parent's constant disapproval. Kids who felt they could never please their parents, their father in particular, often believe that they are a disappointment to God as well. Seeing themselves as defective, unworthy of their father's love, they come to believe that they could never please a Heavenly Father either. And Satan wins. Any time the devil can get us to believe that our Heavenly Father sees us as a disappointment he has effectively created distance between us and God, which is his number one objective.

Believing that we are a disappointment to God causes us to exercise one of two strategies. Dr. Woititz describes it in terms of either becoming "super responsible" or "super irresponsible." Those who are super responsible set out to do whatever it takes to please the Heavenly Father. We just keep performing—doing and saying all the right things to win God's approval. It saddens me to see how many people who have been lifelong Christians still operate under the flagrantly false impression that God's love must be earned. We may tell ourselves it isn't true, we may know that the Bible clearly says it isn't true, yet, at some level, we still believe that it is; we believe that if we can just be "good enough" we can win God's love. That plan didn't work in proving ourselves to our earthly fathers. It's equally futile to believe it will work with our Heavenly Father.

Our good deeds must flow out of a genuine love for and gratefulness to God. Yet, all too often, our efforts are fueled by a fear of disappointing Him and being declared unworthy of His love. Even in terms of Christian service, it is feasible to accomplish really good things and have really bad motives.

It is possible, even if our noble deeds drew the applause of men, and God Himself were to give us a standing ovation, that we would still see ourselves as a disappointment. For super responsible people, no matter how much we've done for God and how well we've done it, the *S* on our chest belies the *L* on our forehead.

At the other end of the spectrum we have the super irresponsible. Those are the people who understand that all their wonderful deeds and accomplishments are for naught. We may have tried for years to win our Heavenly Father's approval but have concluded that we never will. So we stop trying. Some of us take it a step further. Armed with years of frustration and failure, we set out to give God something to be disappointed about. In its subtlest form this acting out can take the form of our adopting a lethargic, "what's the use" attitude. More destructive effects of being super irresponsible include the development of antisocial behaviors. Rather than merely feeling like a disappointment, we feel the need to prove that we are.

Whether the belief that we are displeasing to God propels us toward being super responsible or super irresponsible the end result is the same: distance from our Heavenly Father.

In the Garden of Eden, before sin came into world, Adam and Eve enjoyed an intimate relationship with God. Because neither Adam nor Eve had a father, God became a father to them. He walked with them and talked with them and told them that they were His own. As Rick Warren pointed out in his book *Purpose Driven Life*, "There were no rituals, ceremonies, or religion—just a simple loving relationship between God and the people He created. Unhindered by guilt or fear, Adam and Eve delighted in God, and He delighted in them."

Created For Intimacy

Humankind was created for intimacy with God. The divine intent was that all of God's children bask in a perfect, loving relationship with their Heavenly Father. But that plan bit the dust when Eve bit the apple. Sin left a gaping hole between God and man; a formidable chasm between the created and the Creator. God could have thrown up His hands and walked away. But we mean too much to Him. His desire for intimacy with us is too great. The gap needed to be closed. So He sent His Son to serve as a bridge between us imperfect, sinful children and a Father who loves us anyway. Christ's death on the cross enables all who believe to once again have personal access to the Heavenly Father. Jesus provided, and continues to provide, the only way back to close relationship with God.

The Bible tells us that at the exact moment Jesus died the veil of the temple was split from top to bottom. Don't let the significance of that miracle escape you. The temple, during the time of Jesus, was the hub of Jewish religious life. The temple veil cordoned off the Holy of Holies—God's earthly dwelling place—from the rest of the temple where men were allowed. When we hear the word veil, we most often picture a bridal veil made of thin, transparent fabric. Tearing fabric you can see through isn't much of a miracle. The veil of the temple, however, is estimated by historians to have been close to sixty feet high, thirty feet wide, and four inches thick. The veil symbolized mankind's separation from God by sin. Only one person was allowed access to the Holy of Holies. One time each year, the high priest would enter the presence of God by going beyond the veil to make atonement for the sins of the people.

According to the book of Matthew, the very second Jesus took His last breath on the cross "the curtain of the temple was torn in two from top to bottom" (Matt. 27:51, NLT). Those last four words are particularly significant. The tearing of the veil from top to bottom is conclusive evidence that God was doing the ripping. He removed the barrier, once and for all, between a sinful people and a holy God. The permanent opening of the curtain gives all who believe access once again to a loving Heavenly Father who longs to be close to His kids.

Pleasing God

Though you would never know it by listening to some fathers, there is only one Father who is perfect. This Father's goal for His children is stated in 1 Peter 1:15–16: "Be holy in all you do; for it is written 'Be holy, because I am holy'" (NIV). And you thought your earthly dad had unreasonable expectations. God sets a high standard for His kids not because He takes some sort of twisted pleasure in seeing us fail, but because He wants what is best for us. He knows that none of His children will attain perfection on this earth. But He also knows that the more we exhibit holiness, which is spiritual purity, the less we will experience turmoil and trouble in our lives.

While our Heavenly Father is disappointed in some of our choices and behaviors, that is not the same as being disappointed with or in us. God's disappointment is not with who we are, but in what we sometimes do.

The Bible tells us that sin displeases God to the point that He grieves over it. But our Heavenly Father weeps not because we are missing the mark, but because we are missing His best for us. God, better than anyone, knows our brokenness. He is aware of every issue in our lives that hinders us from being all that we were created to be. More than disappointed, God is pained by the separation from Him that results when we convince ourselves that we are unworthy of His love.

God is pleased with us. Not because of what we've done, but because of who we are—His kids. We were created by Him, designed by Him, and adopted into His family. This is what the Bible tells us:

- "God decided in advance to adopt us into his own family by bringing us to himself through Jesus Christ. This is what he wanted to do, and it gave him great pleasure. So we praise God for the glorious grace he has poured out on us who belong to his dear Son" (Eph. 1:5–6, NLT).

- "Everything that goes into a life of pleasing God has been miraculously given to us by getting to know, personally and intimately, the One who invited us to God" (2 Peter 1:3, MSG).

But there is a stipulation to pleasing our Heavenly Father. We must have faith that He is who He says He is. Hebrews 11:6 states it clearly: "Without faith it is impossible to please God, because anyone who comes to him must believe that he exists and that he rewards those who earnestly seek him" (NIV).

If we believe who God is—infallible, true, perfect in all His ways—then we can be absolutely sure of whom we are—His beloved children with whom He is well pleased.

Knowing Who We Are

In the 1940s, Frank Szymanski, a center for the Notre Dame football team, was called as a witness in a civil suit in South Bend. "Are you on the Notre Dame football team this year?" the judge asked.

Szymanski replied, "Yes, Your Honor."

The judge asked, "What position?"

"Center, Your Honor," came the response.

"How good a center?" asked the judge.

Szymanski squirmed in his seat, then said firmly, "I am the best center Notre Dame ever had."

Coach Frank Leahy, who was in the courtroom, was surprised by the answer of the usually modest, unassuming Szymanski. When the proceedings were over, the coach took Szymanski aside and asked why he made such a statement.

Szymanski blushed and said, "I hated to do it, Coach, but, after all, I was under oath."

Allow me, based on the testimony of Scripture, to tell you the truth and nothing but the truth. You are a beloved child of God.

He treasures you. He actively pursues a relationship with you. He delights in spending time with you. He rejoices over you with singing. He invites you to share with Him your dreams and desires, your problems and pain. He offers you love without condition and grace without exception. He is pleased to call you His own.

The verdict is in, the blood test performed by Jesus Himself: You are a child of the Heavenly Father!

CHAPTER 11

A Father Who Suffers With Us

Christ did not come to do away with suffering.
He did not come to explain it.
He came to fill it with His presence.

Paul Claudel

"How did you feel as you saw your daddy drive away?"

For the first time in the session Dejohn shifted his gaze from the parking lot outside the window to the man who was trying to get inside his pain. Dejohn wasn't sure how to let his words out and keep his tears in. No one had ever asked that question before.

Dejohn was seven years old when he watched his father throw his few belongings into the back of a rusty Chevy and jerk out of the parking space in front of their inner city three-flat. Dejohn's mother stood undaunted on the narrow patch of front lawn, arms folded, screaming for her husband to leave while Dejohn bounced up and down next to the car, arms open, pleading with his daddy to stay. Though he was barefoot and in clear defiance of his mother's demands to go inside, Dejohn ran down the street behind his father's car for almost three blocks, sobbing, "I'm sorry, Daddy. Please don't go."

Throughout his adolescence Dejohn wrestled with a nagging question: What was so wrong with him that his dad never wanted to see him again? Dejohn never verbalized the question. But it was planted deep inside his soul. For twelve years it had produced a fairly consistent crop of bitterness and cynicism, further straining an already precarious home life.

By age fifteen, Dejohn's attitude had pushed his mother to the brink. The resulting ultimatum: either talk with Bishop Thomas "until you're straightened out" or find another place to live. Dejohn didn't like getting preached at while in a congregation of two hundred, let alone being the sole target of the preacher's fire and brimstone. But being subjected to an hour of the bishop's judgment was still a far better option than losing the only parent he had left. Dejohn phoned the church office and made an appointment.

Dejohn's weekly church attendance was non-negotiable. His mother said it at least once every Sunday morning: "You live in my house, you follow my rules." Dejohn hated the marathon church services, made even longer by the lack of air conditioning. He hated getting elbowed by his mother when he dozed off during the insufferably long prayers. Most of all, he hated that there were very few fathers there.

Dejohn didn't talk much in the preacher's office, partly because he didn't want to, but mostly because he didn't have to. Bishop Thomas had already been filled in by Dejohn's mother regarding his "belligerence." If there was another side to the story the preacher had no interest in hearing it. He had no inkling as to what was really going on inside Dejohn's troubled soul but that did not stop him from making an immediate diagnosis: "You have an unforgiving spirit." The bishop's advice was even more simplistic than his assessment: "It is your responsibility as a Christian to forgive your daddy." The bishop's assignment became an ultimatum when he added, "If you don't forgive your daddy, God won't forgive you." The bishop made it known that those were not *his* words; rather, they came directly from the mouth of God. He then pulled a sheet of paper out of his middle desk drawer and handed it to Dejohn. On it was a list of Scripture passages having to do with forgiveness. Dejohn was instructed to memorize them. For good measure, the bishop also told Dejohn that he needed to pray harder.

More out of desperation than obligation, Dejohn actually tried to carry out the bishop's instructions. He knew he hadn't forgiven his father. He knew he wasn't as close to God as he should be. But following the preacher's surefire formula didn't fix his problems. If anything, it only made matters worse.

No Easy Fix

A couple years later, Dejohn befriended a young lady who was in his biology class. Jasmine saw Dejohn as a diamond in the rough. She appreciated and affirmed the good she saw in him—his inquisitive nature, his compassionate heart, and his sense of humor—but she was honest with him that she had some concerns that prevented them from ever becoming more than study buddies. He had a hair trigger temper, and even though the target of his wrath was almost always himself, his random explosions made her very uncomfortable. Likewise, she didn't appreciate his sarcastic jokes, even though he made them at his own expense.

She cared enough for Dejohn to recommend he make an appointment with her friend's father, who was a Christian counselor. He agreed, primarily because he saw it as hurdle in the race to her heart. In preparation for his appointment with Mr. Trenton, Dejohn reviewed the bishop's easy steps to emotional and spiritual wellness—he made sure he was all prayed up and he reviewed the Bible passages the bishop made him memorize. Just in case the bishop and the counselor were in cahoots, he wanted to be prepared if there was some sort of quiz.

Dejohn stared out the window as he offered Mr. Trenton the perfunctory thumbnail sketch of his life. When he was finished he expected the counselor to make his judgment, give him a to-do list, and send him on his way. Instead, Dejohn's story was met with several seconds of awkward, yet strangely engaging silence before the counselor said softly, "You were seven years old! How did you feel when you stood barefoot in the street that day and watched your daddy drive away?" For the first time in his life, Dejohn didn't feel alone. Finally, there was someone who wanted to enter his suffering. Once the therapist nudged the door open Dejohn immediately slid the chain off the latch and opened it wide.

For the next several sessions Dejohn cried tears of sadness over not having a father to love him, tears of guilt over things he did (real or perceived) that might have caused his dad to leave, tears of shame over not "being good enough" to make his father want to stay, tears of bitterness over not having control over the situation, and tears of anger over dads in general who blow off their responsibilities. Child abuse is often defined in terms of demonstrative physical or verbal outbursts. Yet Dejohn is one of countless children who have been deeply wounded by a parent's indifference.

There aren't many beliefs as devastating to a person's healing process than the conclusion that God couldn't care less.

Just when Dejohn thought there were no tears left, more would come. But at the core of the sadness, guilt, shame, bitterness, and anger was a deeper issue that would have remained untouched were it not for Mr. Trenton's persistent prodding. Buried under all the debris was a foundational fear: Dejohn was afraid that His Heavenly Father didn't care about him either. There aren't many beliefs as devastating to a person's healing process than the conclusion that God couldn't care less.

God's Indifference

Dr. Myron J. Taylor once wrote, "The real sting of suffering is not misfortune itself, nor even the pain or the *injustice of it*, but the apparent God-forsakenness of it. Pain is endurable, but the seeming indifference of God is not." [17]

I have always believed in God. But the God I knew as a child had come from the same mold as my father. Consequently, while I never doubted my Heavenly Father's existence, I had serious reservations about His being concerned about me and the volatile environment I was living in. I believed the Heavenly Father *could* do something about my dad's drinking. I believed He *could* do something about my fear and sadness. But He didn't. He had chosen to look the other way. I knew that the Heavenly Father had the capacity to love me but concluded that He had decided not to.

I felt the same about my Heavenly Father that I did about my earthly father—that He didn't care about me. As if feeling disconnected from God wasn't hurtful enough, I could envision Him twirling the plug in His fingers. Try as I might, it was impossible to have an exuberant faith in an apathetic God. Believe me, there is no more disheartening, deflating feeling than that of God's being disinterested in us.

> **Try as I might, it was impossible to have an exuberant faith in an apatheticGod.**

Years ago, when I shared with my pastor friend how God's seeming indifference toward me placed an insurmountable barrier between me and my Heavenly Father, he asked a rather interesting question: "How do you feel about Jesus?"

A smile brightened my face. "We're like this," I said, holding up two intertwined fingers. "Jesus was persecuted, He felt like an outcast, He was misunderstood even by the people closest to Him, people talked about Him behind His back, He felt rejected. Yeah, that Guy I can relate to!"

The pastor mirrored my smile. "Then that's the Guy you need to pray to. You need to pray to Jesus until you realize that He and the Father are the same person."

I had a solid connection with God the Son. Jesus *got* me. If anyone could relate to what I was going through, it was Him. God the Son knew better than anyone what it was like to live a life of pain and persecution. He died due to the hurtful, hateful acts of others. The prophet Isaiah offers this character sketch of God the Son: "He was despised and rejected by mankind, a man of suffering, and familiar with pain. Like one from whom people hide their faces he was despised, and we held him in low esteem" (Is. 53:3, NIV). Jesus didn't just *experience* suffering. He was a *man of suffering.*

Which of the following experiences might you and God the Son have in common?

- Jesus was rejected by the people closest to Him.

- He was misunderstood.

- He was hurt by people's refusal to admit they were wrong.

- He was laughed at and made fun of.

- He was criticized when He hadn't done anything wrong.

- He was hurt when people He cared about made poor choices.

- He was deceived by "friends."

- He couldn't do enough to please certain people (and He was perfect!).

- He was second-guessed.

- He experienced anger when people minimized Him.

- His own family members didn't believe in Him.

- He was mocked and ridiculed.

- People questioned his motives.

- His closest friends didn't always trust Him to do what He said
  He'd do.

- He was often in situations where He had to prove Himself.

- The good things He did were often overlooked.

- He was hated.

- He was abused.

God the Son was a man of suffering; an identity He willingly took on because He cares so deeply about us. Isaiah explains: "[But] he was pierced for our rebellion, crushed for our sins. He was beaten so we could be whole. He was whipped so we could be healed" (Is. 53:5, NLT).

The Suffering Servant

While Jesus can relate to our suffering, we can't possibly relate to His. Jesus experienced incomprehensible pain before and during His death on the cross. The word *excruciating* is derived from the Latin *excruciatus* which means *out of the cross*. Death by crucifixion was not just agonizing, it was disgraceful. It was generally reserved for the vilest of criminals. Roman jurist Julius Paulus listed crucifixion as the worst of all capital punishments, above being burned alive and being beheaded.

The Roman soldiers positioned Jesus on the cross in such a way as to cause maximum suffering. In order to take a breath, Jesus had to lift His body by pushing up on His feet and bending His elbows, putting full pressure on the nail wounds in His wrists and feet. The resulting pain was like an electrical shock throughout His body. His inability to breathe properly resulted in throbbing muscle cramps. His back, still bearing open wounds from the whipping, scraped against the rough, wooden beam every time He straightened His body to inhale.

Breathing was difficult enough; speaking took determined effort. Yet Jesus mustered up what faint strength He had left because He had to say something. It was not a request for mercy, despite the searing physical pain. It was not a complaint, though His suffering was beyond comprehension. He didn't direct a curse toward the men holding the hammers, though His punishment was undeserved. Those things weren't the most important to Jesus. The Man of Suffering had to speak what was foremost on His heart. God the Son not only cried out, but cried with a loud voice, "My God, my God, why have you forsaken me?" (Matt. 27:46, NIV)

His accusers spit in His face. He was stripped naked and tortured. The sinless Son of God was crucified like a common criminal. Yet the single most painful indignity Jesus suffered was the feeling of being forsaken by His own Father. It was easier for Him to bear unspeakable physical torture than the thought that His Father had turned His face away.

Forsaken

I have heard the life stories of people who, as young children, were the innocent victims of satanic sexual ritual abuse whose own fathers were among the perpetrators. As adults, they struggle to try to make sense out of what had happened to them; things that are truly senseless. Perhaps the single biggest hindrance to their healing is the belief that no one can relate. Family members, in an effort to protect the family secret, make them out to be liars. Friends, who can't allow themselves to believe that such evil exists, choose to keep their distance. Others give the appearance of being supportive, but their raised eyebrows give them away. Uninformed church members and clueless clergy often play the grace card. They don't understand or want to understand what happened. They simply nod unknowingly, offering their mantra, "God's grace is sufficient."

So in many instances, the abused are left to go it alone, convinced that no one could understand—not even Jesus. They reason that while the Son of God may have a divine capacity for empathy, He can't possibly feel what they feel. They acknowledged that while Jesus may have had to deal with many different kinds of pain in His life, He has no clue what it's like to be raped by His own father in the name of Satan and then be left alone to wrestle with the demons of shame and guilt for the rest of His days.

The reality is that those who have experienced such evil abuse do have something in common with Jesus. He felt forsaken by His father, too. He also experienced that ice cold separation from the One who gave Him life. The Son of God understands what it feels like to be all alone. The moment He wailed, "My God, my God, why have you forsaken me," He sealed a bond with every person who ever felt abused and abandoned by his or her father.

Adding further significance to Jesus's cry from the cross is that He didn't refer to His Father as *Father*. Jesus always called God *Father*. But in this moment of soul wrenching separation anxiety, He couldn't even bring Himself to use the word. The earthly torment of God's Son culminated in the most wretched pain of all: the unbearably lonely feeling of separation from His Dad.

Every single hurt Jesus felt while on this earth He bore for us. He willingly took on the full weight of our sin—including the sense of separation from God the Father that sin always brings. 2 Corinthians 5:21 says, "For God made Christ, who never sinned, to be the offering for our sin so that we could be made right with God through Christ" (NLT). The cross of Jesus stands as the pinnacle of

> **The earthly torment of God's Son culminated in the most wretched pain of all: the unbearably lonely feeling of separation from His Dad.**

our Heavenly Father's love for us. Nowhere is God's suffering for

His children so powerfully and painfully displayed as at the cross of Calvary.

The Wordless Sermon

During the Middle Ages, a monk one day announced that he would be presenting a sermon that evening on the love of God. People gathered in the cathedral as the sun was setting. They stood in silence as the last gasps of sunlight breathed through the heavy, wood-framed windows. When darkness had settled over the sanctuary the monk entered. Taking a lighted candle from the massive candelabrum he walked past the altar to the life-sized statue of Jesus on the cross, a figure that presided over every mass. In silence, the monk held the light beneath the wounds on Jesus' feet. After several seconds, he raised the candle and paused by Jesus's hands. He then brought the candle down to Jesus's sword-punctured side. After a few moments, still without a word, he raised the candle to allow its light to shine on the Savior's thorn-crowned brow.

The silence of the monk's wordless sermon was broken by the sounds of weeping from many in the darkened church. Those assembled that night experienced like never before the mystery of the love of God—a love so deeply profound that words cannot begin to describe it.

Suffering With Us

When God became flesh, He willingly laid aside His immunity to pain. He suffered for us. But, what's more, He suffers *with* us.

Let the biblical record show—the world God created for His children was perfect. Our first parents, Adam and Eve, enjoyed a pain-free, problem-free existence. Imagine a world with no cavities or creditors, no dandelions or dumb drivers, no cigarette smoke or spam, no bad breath or busy signals, no mosquito bites or milk that tastes funny, no colonoscopies or country music (okay, that's *my* idea of paradise). Adam and Eve lived in a perfect world, in perfect relationship with a perfect Heavenly Father who loved them perfectly. But then came sin. Adam and Eve's willful disobedience changed everything. If they had any comprehension what their taste for forbidden fruit would lead to, they would have opted for the calorie-free chocolate (it was a perfect world, remember?). God's brilliant blueprint now had a sin stain all over it.

It's a common reaction to blame God when our lives don't go according to plan. It's easy to see Him as the enemy, as if He caused our misfortune or, at the very least, didn't do anything to prevent it. But we don't experience suffering in this world because of God, we experience suffering because of sin.

God is not our enemy, He is our ally. Our Heavenly Father, the Man of Suffering, sides with us. Whenever our pillow is wet with tears, we can be assured that our Father in Heaven cries right with us. He is not an uninvolved bystander. He is not emotionally disconnected when His children are hurting. He suffers with us. He hurts when we hurt. He has deep concern for His kids.

> **Whenever our pillow is wet with tears, we can be assured that our Father in Heaven cries right with us.**

In His book *The Prophets,* Jewish scholar Abraham Heschel writes, "The most exalted idea applied to God is not infinite wisdom, infinite power, but infinite concern." He is a Father who cares.

A Loss to be Grieved

The book of Lamentations, as the title suggests, is an expression of suffering. It is often referred to as the book of tears. It was written by Jeremiah, who was known as the weeping prophet. Lamentations is the verbalization of Jeremiah's broken heart. He was hurt by the sinful and selfish behavior of others. He writes of being distressed, disturbed, and bitter. Jeremiah's journal includes his confession of feeling rejected and alone. He wonders aloud if there is any suffering like the suffering he is experiencing. He laments, "No one is near to comfort me, no one to restore my spirit" (Lam. 1:16, NIV). The book of Lamentations is a manual on grief.

It is unfortunate that, as mentioned in chapter two, we tend to think of grieving only in terms of losing a loved one. There are many losses in life that must be grieved—the loss of a job, the loss of a marriage, the loss of health, the loss of ability.

Another significant loss that must be grieved, yet often isn't, is the loss of a childhood.

Another significant loss that must be grieved, yet often isn't, is the loss of a childhood. A growing number of people, through no fault of their own, did not have much of a childhood: kids of alcoholics, kids of abusers, kids of parents who are mentally ill, kids of divorce, kids who don't even know who their father is. Due to the upheaval of the family structure in our society, countless children have had to become adults at a very early age. Losing our childhood is a tremendous loss, yet because many of us simply accept our circumstances as normal, we never really grieve the loss.

Grief Defined

The definition of the word grief is *the expression of intense, mental anguish.* The key word in that summation is *expression.* If we are not expressing our anguish, we are not grieving. For us to truly grieve, those intense feelings need to come out. When we read Lamentations, it is clear that Jeremiah was a man who knew how to grieve.

Whatever loss we are suffering—the loss of security, the loss of innocence, the loss of a dream, the loss of an ideal—it is important for us to grieve. We must recognize the severity of our loss, acknowledge and validate our feelings surrounding the loss, then express those feelings. That is what happens when we grieve. We cannot grieve as long as we deny our anguish or refuse to let it go. And until we grieve we will never find complete healing from our wounds. God promises to heal the broken-hearted and bind up our wounds (Ps. 34:18). That cannot happen if we never admit that we've been wounded.

> **We cannot grieve as long as we deny our anguish or refuse to let it go.**

Our personal recovery from painful childhood losses can begin once we dislodge the emotions that have been mired for years in our souls and then express those feelings in healthy ways. Trudging through the grieving process is not for the faint of heart. The anguish caused by suppressed feelings may be excruciating. But it is not until we feel those feelings all the way through that we can put them behind us.

Providing great comfort, however, is understanding that we never grieve alone. Our Heavenly Father grieves with us.

As Jeremiah went through the grieving process, he, much like David did in the book of Psalms, struggled with what God's role was in his suffering. And even though God was, at times, a target of Jeremiah's anger, the prophet recognized his Heavenly Father as his sole source of healing. After unleashing his intense anguish Jeremiah wrote, "Because of the LORD's great love we are not consumed, for his compassions never fail. They are new every morning. The LORD is good to those whose hope is in him, to the one who seeks him; it is good to wait quietly for the salvation of the LORD" (Lam. 3:22–23, 25–26, NIV).

We must seek God always, but especially in tough times. The Heavenly Father assured Jeremiah and promises us: [Then] you will call on me and come and pray to me, and I will listen to you. You will seek me and find me when you seek me with all your heart" (Jer. 29:12-13, NIV).

We must look to God for help in the healing process. We may need to ask Him to reveal more of His caring nature to us, to prove to us that He understands; that He is an ally in our suffering and that He wants to deliver us. If we seek Him with all our heart, we will find Him.

There are three places to look when seeking God. We find Him in His Word, in prayer, and in His people.

Seeking God in His Word

Unlike most every movie produced by Disney, the main character of the Bible is a present and loving Father. Every frame of Scripture works together to draw a picture of a Heavenly Father who lovingly pursues a relationship with us, His children.

The Bible also graphically illustrates God's greatness. When we ponder that particular attribute of God we tend to focus on His creation. After all, He carved the Grand Canyon, designed DNA, and painted the planets. But the case can be made that nowhere is God's greatness more readily seen than in His faithfulness to His children. Our Heavenly Father is faithful in His love for His kids.

If it is true that one cannot love without being vulnerable and that being vulnerable involves opening oneself to pain, then it stands to reason that since God loves us He also suffers with us. If we feel alone in our suffering, it indicates that we still haven't found what we're looking for—a Father who cares. May I remind you again: *If we seek the Heavenly Father with all our heart we will find Him.* Allow Him to introduce Himself to you through His Word. You will find that He is faithful and merciful; He is gracious and good; He is all-knowing and all-powerful; He is ever present and never changes. But, most of all, you will discover how much He loves you. And because He loves you He longs to enter your suffering so that your wounds may be healed.

Seeking God in Prayer

Another vehicle that transports us directly to God's residence is prayer. Since He resides in the hearts of those who believe, we won't need a GPS to find Him. David assures us, "The LORD is near to all who call on him, to all who call on him in truth" (Ps. 145:18, NIV). Isaiah encourages us, "Seek the LORD while he may be found; call on him while he is near" (Is. 55:6, NIV).

Despite this being a technological age, I find communication between humans to be increasingly difficult. I'm not one to live in the past, but I pine for the days of yesteryear when you could inquire about your business accounts via telephone and, without pressing any additional numbers, actually speak to a real, live person. I don't find communicating online to be much easier. I shouldn't have to divulge my social security number, share my mother's maiden name, and turn my head and cough just to get my checking account balance.

It's refreshing to know that we have instant access to our Heavenly Father. There are no codes to enter or passwords to remember. We won't get a busy signal or a recorded message. We call; He answers. It is against God's nature to not be available to us when we call.

> **It is against God's nature to not be available to us when we call.**

"Let us then approach God's throne of grace with confidence, so that we may receive mercy and find grace to help us in our time of need" (Heb. 4:16, NIV).

Seeking God in His People

While we can readily find God in His Word and in prayer, there are times—especially when our suffering is immense—that we need to see Him in people. Many of us have heard the story of a little boy who was afraid of the dark who found no comfort in his parent's assurance that "God would always be there." He cried out, "But I need God with skin on!"

Sometimes we need God with skin on. As assuring and comforting as reading His Word and praying is, God often works most powerfully through His people. I'm not saying that Bible reading and prayer won't help someone who has been abused or abandoned by their father, but their chances of finding healing for their father wounds are infinitely greater if they are *shown* the love of the Heavenly Father in relationships with God's people. Like Dejohn needed to experience the love of his Heavenly Father through a godly counselor like Mr. Trenton, sometimes God is most readily found in His people.

When working through our father wounds we must surround ourselves with safe, trustworthy people who genuinely want God's best for us.

I encourage those who are suffering loss to build as big a support base as they can. The more loving, encouraging people there are in our support network the greater the likelihood we will find the healing we need. When working through our father wounds we must surround ourselves with safe, trustworthy people who genuinely want God's best for us. Our support base may include good friends, mentors, coaches, youth leaders, or pastors. In some cases, it is necessary to solicit the help of a professional therapist.

Thankfully, the stigma of seeing a counselor is fading in our culture. While some may still look at seeing a therapist as a sign of weakness, I see it as a sign of strength. It takes a strong person to admit that something is wrong in our life and be willing to do whatever it takes to make it right.

Sometimes it takes a while to find the right therapist. I have suggested to a number of people that they seek the help of a professional counselor only to have them say, "I tried counseling. It didn't work." The fact is, sometimes it doesn't work. But a failed counseling experience is most often the result of a personality clash, our inability to trust, or a poor fit in terms of the counselor's gender, age, or area of expertise. None of those things warrant the conclusion that counseling doesn't work. They only indicate that we haven't found the right counselor. If we brought our car in to a mechanic who wasn't able to fix it we wouldn't throw up our hands and say, "Well, I tried. I guess I'll have to walk to work every day." We would find another mechanic. If your therapist is not helping, and you are doing your part in the process, you need to find another therapist.

The same can be said for our friends—they need to be chosen wisely. We may have had a father who was caustic, opinionated, and demeaning. We can't choose our fathers. But we can choose our friends. In one of his meditations, author William Arthur Ward once wrote, "A true friend knows your weaknesses but shows you your strengths; feels your fears but fortifies your faith; sees your anxieties but frees your spirit; recognizes your disabilities but emphasizes your possibilities."

Some of the people we surround ourselves with take us by the hand and walk with us down the road to recovery. Some take us by the arm and pull us into the ditch of despair. The friends we choose to include in our support network must be like God in that they have our best interests in mind. If we are committed to discovering the love, healing, and grace of our Heavenly Father through relationship with His Son, we need to place ourselves in the company of friends who want the same thing for us. We need friends who are encouraging, inspiring, and life-giving; friends who shine like Jesus and who help us to shine like Jesus. We can't seek to live in the Son and hang around shady people. (And, no, I do not give churches permission to put that quote on their signs.)

> We can't seek to live in the Son and hang around shady people.

George Washington was dead-on when he said, "It's better to be alone than in bad company." Or, to quote wise King Solomon, "The righteous choose their friends carefully, but the way of the wicked leads them astray" (Prov. 12:26, TNIV).

God has provided me with a number of helpers as I have sought healing from my father wounds. I have benefitted from sessions with excellent therapists, from long talks with empathetic friends; I have been enlightened by the words of various authors and have been challenged by powerful speakers. All have facilitated my recovery and strengthened my faith. But the single greatest "aha" moment in my journey toward healing took place in the context of a support group.

The therapist I was seeing at a Christian counseling agency (where I was later blessed to be on staff) encouraged me to join a Tuesday night ACOA (Adult Children of Alcoholics) group. I won't soon forget the night when I trusted the group enough to share my story. I sensed that they would care, even though I was convinced they would never understand. As I spoke of my father's wanton drinking and the abuse that resulted, I could see rhythmic movement in my peripheral vision. I looked around the room to see every head nodding. They understood me! Though our stories were different, the injustices we suffered were the same. I wasn't alone after all.

Find a support group. Whether it is a recovery group, a church small group, or a twelve-step group, it is imperative that we become a part of a network of supportive friends. Look for a group whose focus is on recovery. We may want to seek a group led by a professional counselor. Without good leadership, a group can easily lose its focus. I have visited a number of groups that were nothing more than glorified gripe sessions, where people were not all that interested in solutions and instead, just wanted to hash and rehash their problems. If a group is not helping us to get where we need to go, we need to find another group.

A support group will be more effective if it includes people who have already experienced the healing we're looking for. A support group will be more effective if it includes people who have already experienced the healing we're looking for. Good support groups help us in rolling up our shirtsleeves to do the dirty work needed to achieve a healthy sense of self-worth. Good support groups help us to grapple with real-life issues like shame, boundaries, communication, identity, and control. Good support groups offer the serenity of a pat on the back, the courage from a kick in the butt, and the wisdom to know when to offer each.

Hand in Hand

Our Heavenly Father is not indifferent to our suffering. He seeks to enter it. He desires to rebuild our broken lives. He provides us with the necessary tools to repair the damage caused by our past, to fortify us to withstand the everyday wear and tear of the present, and to secure a strong future built on the unshakeable foundation of His promises. No matter where we are on the path toward peace and prosperity our Heavenly Father walks with us, hand in hand.

The story is told of a man who was going through a very difficult time in his life. His world seemed to be caving in around him. His problems began to affect him spiritually. One day he shared his troubles with his father, with whom he was blessed to have a good relationship. As he spoke of his distress, his emotions began to get the best of him. He began to sob as he asked, "How can God say he loves me and then allow all this to happen?"

The man's father wisely let him get it all out. He then looked into his son's eyes and said, "Son, do you remember when you were eight years old and you broke your leg?" His son nodded. The father said, "I picked you up, carried you to the car, and raced you to the hospital. You were in such pain. I carried you into the emergency room and waited with you for the doctor to examine you. I tried to assure you that everything was going to be alright."

"The doctor had your leg x-rayed, then called me aside. He told me that your leg was broken and that before a cast could be put on, the bone would have to be set. He said that it would be a very painful procedure." The father continued, "I could have stopped him right there and said, 'my son has suffered enough. I will not allow you to cause him any more pain.' But I knew that for your leg to be healed you were going to have to go through it."

"I'm sure you weren't even aware of it, but as the doctor was setting your leg, and you were crying out in pain, I was standing by your side, crying with you, holding your hand."

That is what our Heavenly Father does when we suffer. When we hurt because we feel lonely, insignificant, rejected, or forsaken, we have a loving Father who stands by our side, crying with us, holding our hand.

CHAPTER 12

A Father Who Gives Us Hope

No man is beaten until his hope is annihilated, his confidence gone.
As long as a man faces life hopefully, confidently, triumphantly,
he is not a failure; he is not beaten until he turns his back on life.

Orison Swett Marden

Luke Skywalker had Darth Vader. Batman had the Joker. For Harry Potter it was Lord Voldemort, and for Popeye it was Bluto. Every hero has an archenemy, an opponent who seeks to bring him harm and ruin. Who is your greatest enemy? Your immediate answer may be, "my father" or the far too obvious, "Satan." But I want you to give it some thought. If you had to name the one person who stands in the way of your living a life of peace, joy, prosperity, and hope, who would it be?

Some of us who have been around long enough to remember hula hoops and Garfield Goose may recall a comic strip called *Pogo*. From 1948 till 1975, many daily newspapers included the philosophical meanderings of Pogo Possum. I am not all that familiar with Pogo. I generally hand the comics to my wife on my way to the sports section. But I am familiar with a quote from Pogo, originally uttered in 1971, because it has become a cultural cliché. Though he is rarely cited, it was indeed Pogo Possum who first said, "We have met the enemy and the enemy is us."

It is true that the devil is our archenemy. It is true that, for many, our father is more an adversary than an ally in our lives. But it is also true that we look into the face of the primary source of harm and ruin in our lives every time we brush our teeth. What *we* think of ourselves and our circumstances will prove a more formidable barrier to a life of hope and healing than anything anyone else could possibly do or say to us. *We* are often our greatest enemy.

Author Thomas Sikking says it succinctly: "You're not the product of a broken home, a devastated economy, a world in the upheaval of war, a minority group, a family of drunkards or a poverty-ridden neighborhood. You are the product of your own thinking processes and whatever you're thinking about today is the cornerstone of your tomorrow."

"Stinkin' thinkin'" as it's called in the world of recovery fills our minds with despair and drains our lives of hope. Children who are raised in dysfunctional environments are often plagued by unhealthy thought patterns well into their adult lives. What is actually true about us and our situation is easily dismissed in favor of what we perceive to be true.

Logic and reason are hijacked by stinkin' thinkin.' This happens in a number of ways:

We adopt an all or nothing mindset. Everything becomes either black or white. People are either for us or against us. Our days are either fantastic or horrible. We are either successful or an abysmal failure.

We expect the worst. Even when there is no basis for our conclusions, we anticipate a negative result. We are convinced that people don't like us, that we will fail the test, that we won't attain success.

We overgeneralize. An indication that we may be guilty of overgeneralizations is our use of the words *always* and *never*. *I can* never *catch a break. I* always *make wrong choices. I will* never *find happiness.*

We magnify our problems. We tell ourselves that no one has the problems we have, that no one could understand what we are going through, that we have been sentenced to a life of misery and disappointment with no chance of parole.

We jump to conclusions. We can't delineate between making a mistake and being a mistake, between failing and being a failure, between doing bad things and being a bad person.

We focus on the negative. We may receive dozens of compliments on the job we did but we obsess for days over the comments of the one person who was mildly critical.

We take on blame. We hold ourselves personally and fully responsible for things that, more times than not, aren't even in our control. As a child, we may have believed that our dad wouldn't have left if we were just a better son or daughter. As an adult, we take on blame— even when it is unwarranted—when it squarely belongs on spouses, friends, coworkers, bosses, or others.

We are as healthy as our thoughts. Stinkin' thinkin' erodes our well-being. It harms us and our relationships. That is why our Heavenly Father prescribes for us, through the apostle Paul, this remedy: "You'll do best by filling your minds and meditating on things true, noble, reputable, authentic, compelling, gracious—the best, not the worst; the beautiful, not the ugly; things to praise, not things to curse" (Phil. 4:8, MSG).

Since we are products of our thinking we'll do best by meditating on thoughts that are beautiful. There is nothing beautiful about a thought life marked by bitterness and blame, negativity and shame. Stinkin' thinkin' does not bring out the best in us, let alone help us to experience God's best for us. Our Heavenly Father has a plan for His kids. It's a plan to make us prosper. It's a plan that points to a promising future. It's a plan that gives us hope. Often the only thing standing in the way of God's plan unfolding in our lives is us.

A Life Without Hope

Brandon had a lot going for him. He just couldn't see it. He was handsome, talented, and sensitive to boot. The girls at his high school dreamed of one day bearing his children. His astonishing good looks were made even more attractive by his being oblivious to them. All Brandon could see when he looked at his reflection was the scar above his chin, a mark that was undetectable even to the people closest to him. To Brandon, it was a gaping wound that exposed his deepest shame.

Although he was considered by others to be personable, Brandon's social charm was often kept at bay by snarling spells of self-loathing. Brandon was a record-setting athlete but could never meet the goals he had set for himself. Brandon possessed a natural acting ability, but his best work was not performed on the high school stage, but rather in the hallways where every day he pretended to have his life together. Brandon believed in God, he just didn't think God believed in him.

Brandon remembered his parents' relationship as being bipolar, vacillating by the minute between bliss and blight. On several occasions his parents' arguing would reach the decibel level that necessitated him and his sisters running from room to room closing the windows so the neighborhood peace would not be disturbed.

Brandon was exactly nine years old when his dad left. He would never forget the date of his dad's departure because it happened just a few hours after Brandon blew out the candles on his birthday cake. He had come out of his bedroom after he was awakened by the yelling. His plan was to ask for a glass of water, the only way a nine year old knew how to defuse a grown-up situation. The fight was so furious his parents didn't even notice him standing next to the counter. His father shook both fists in the direction of his mother and screamed something like, "I'm out of here." With that declaration he spun around to make good on his word and accidentally pushed

Brandon chin first into the cabinet. When his dad bent down to apologize, Brandon's mother screamed, "Haven't you done enough? Just leave him alone." He did. He never spoke to his son again.

For the next eight years Brandon managed to conceal—behind a fake smile and shallow accomplishments—his hurt toward his father, his resentment toward his mother, and his anger toward God. His best friends had no clue. Then, on the night of his seventeenth birthday, Brandon left the house, walked three blocks down the street, and sat on the railroad tracks until the freight train came to take his pain away.

At his memorial service, Brandon's pastor poignantly shared with an audience made up mostly of despondent, disbelieving teens that there are few things more tragic than a life without hope. Brandon's life changed when his father left him. But Brandon's life ended when hope left him.

Choosing Hope

Hope is essential to healing. Hopelessness keeps us sick. Hope keeps us driving forward even when the road is steep. Hopelessness has two gears—neutral and reverse. Hope is a cocoon that nourishes and nurtures and leads to life. Hopelessness is a web that entangles and endangers and leads to death.

Italian author Dante, in his epic poem *Inferno*, opines that the sign above hell reads: *Abandon all hope ye who enter here*. Many of us live in that hell. Worry, fear, and hopelessness are tools of the devil. If Satan can infiltrate our minds and coerce us into thinking that we are doomed to live out our days on this earth in tribulation and despair, he will have essentially alienated us from God's message of hope. The devil knows better than anyone that we will never experience hope as long as we have one leg shackled to yesterday's regrets and the other bound to tomorrow's worries.

Bible teacher and author Warren Wiersbe once said, "Nothing paralyzes our lives like the attitude that things can never change. We need to remind ourselves that God can change things. Outlook determines outcome. If we see only the problems, we will be defeated;

We will remain hopeless as long as we believe we are helpless.

but if we see the possibilities in the problems, we can have victory." We must stop being our own worst enemy. We must flush our minds of stinkin' thinkin'. We will remain hopeless as long as we believe we are helpless.

The Blame Game

Playing the role of a victim has become quite common in our culture. If you are not convinced this victim mindset is running rampant in our society, consider this news story out of Arkansas. A man from Little Rock was awarded $14,500 plus medical expenses after being bitten in the behind by his next door neighbor's beagle. The judgment is rather curious considering the dog was on a chain in its owner's fenced yard. The man who was bitten was only awarded $14,500 and not the much higher figure he was hoping for because the jury believed that the beagle may have been acting in self-defense at the time of the butt bite, considering the bitee had climbed over the fence into his neighbor's yard and had been repeatedly shooting the dog with a pellet gun.

Accepting personal responsibility seems to have gone the way of leisure suits and disco balls. More and more people, when things go wrong in their lives, feel a need to place blame anywhere but on themselves. Every day in offices across our land, clergy and counselors are subjected to comments like:

- *With parents like mine how can I ever be successful?*

- *He's the reason I drink so much.*

- *If she paid more attention to me I wouldn't have to look elsewhere to get my needs met.*

- *Thanks to him I'll never be happy again.*

- *How can I be a good father when I didn't have a good father?*

When we insist on seeing ourselves as victims, hope will always be just outside our grasp. Most of us don't want to hear it, but the truth of the matter is, no one has the power to make us angry, hurt, or depressed unless we give them

> **When we insist on seeing ourselves as victims, hope will always be just outside our grasp.**

that power. No one has the power to ruin our day, let alone destroy our life. Our fathers may have fouled up our past, but their ruining our present and our future can only happen with our permission.

Recovering from father wounds is a process that involves identifying and expressing our feelings, one at a time. However, feelings like dejection, disappointment, and discouragement will never fully dissipate until we first reconcile the feeling of hopelessness. There is no point in seeking to resolve our sadness, anger, or fearfulness if we have no hope that better things await us. Healing and hopelessness cannot coexist.

Forgiveness

Nothing will short-circuit our recovery process and guarantee our staying stuck in hopelessness more than a lack of forgiveness. When we, either verbally or in our mind, make the vow, "I will never forgive you," we have placed hope and peace on the altar of resentment and revenge.

Here's a news flash: Our fathers may never change. They may continue in their dysfunction until the day they die. They may never come to the point where they acknowledge they did anything wrong, let alone say they're sorry. We need to forgive them anyway. And not because *they* deserve it, but because *we* deserve it.

Tim learned this at an early age. In his last year of high school, Tim, knowing his dad would not be happy about it, made the decision to seek a degree in youth ministry. Tim began a new relationship with God while at a youth retreat. That weekend ignited in him a passion to help young people experience the love, healing, and grace he had come to experience in his newfound relationship with God. But Tim's father served a different God. A self-made millionaire, Tim's dad had committed his life to amassing wealth. His plans were for his son to make it a family venture.

"You want to do what?" Tim's father was incredulous. "How do you expect to make a living being a youth pastor? There's no money in it! Go ahead and throw your life away, but don't expect any help from me."

Tim struggled for years to pay off his student loans. But surrendering sleep and a social life in order to work side jobs was not his most difficult challenge in earning his youth ministry degree. The harder struggle was forgiving his father. Tim expected his dad's cold shoulder, but he was devastated by his father's cold heart. Years after earning his degree and sacrificing much to pay for it, the passing of his grandmother led Tim to make an unsettling discovery. His grandma, a fellow Christian who was thrilled with his career choice, had, without his knowing, set up an education fund to help pay for his schooling. Tim didn't know about it because his father, under the guise of helping Tim's grandmother with her finances, managed to reroute the funds to his own account, secretly swindling his son out of every cent.

A paper trail was found that would have made for a slam dunk lawsuit against his dad, but after much prayer and soul searching Tim determined that no amount of money that would come from a favorable verdict was enough to cover the emotional expense of seeing his father on the witness stand, trying to justify stealing from his son. The money could have allowed Tim to move out of his studio apartment and buy a townhome. But rather than seek a higher standard of living, Tim sought to live to a higher standard. Tim decided that instead of pursuing justice he needed to pursue forgiveness. Without it, he would be forever chained to his dad and drained of hope. Eventually, Tim was able to forgive his father. But their relationship was unalterably changed.

"Forgiveand forget" is another one of those phrases that people think is scriptural, but is not. While the Bible tells us that God forgets our sins and remembers them no more (Heb. 10:17), we mortals are not held to that same standard. Our brains do not come equipped with a delete button. We may be able to move mental files to the recycle bin but they are never fully erased. But while we are not expected to forget, we are commanded by God to forgive. To add an exclamation point to God's command, Jesus Himself stipulates what will happen if we don't forgive: "For if you forgive other people when they sin against you, your Heavenly Father will also forgive you. But if you do not forgive others their sins, your Father will not forgive your sins" (Matt. 6:14–15, NIV).

Forgiving others is not optional, no matter what their offense. In our culture forgiving someone who has wronged us is seen as a weakness; as

> **Forgiving others is not optional, no matter what their offense.**

giving in to our offender. In the eyes of our Heavenly Father, however, forgiveness is a sign of spiritual strength. Forgiveness is not giving in to people who do us wrong; it is giving up the right to hold onto resentment toward them. Forgiveness gives closure to pain and gives wings to hope.

When we forgive others, no matter how deep the wounds they have inflicted and regardless of whether or not they ever admit to any wrong doing, we are poised to receive healing. When we choose to forgive, the embers of hope embedded in our soul are fanned into flame.

The God of Hope

God is a Father who blesses His children with hope—so much so that Scripture refers to Him as the *God of hope.* Jeremiah writes, "Blessed are those who trust in the LORD and have made the LORD their hope and confidence. They are like trees planted along a riverbank, with roots that reach deep into the water. Such trees are not bothered by the heat or worried by long months of drought. Their leaves stay green, and they never stop producing fruit" (Jer. 17:7–8, NLT).

Just before Jeremiah wrote these words of blessing, he warned of a curse: "Cursed is the one who trusts in man" (v. 5). We cannot pin our hopes for a better life on counselors, spouses, employers—even presidents. Our hope is not dependent on our father's sobri-

Our hope is not dependent on our father's sobriety, recovery, or apology.

ety, recovery, or apology. We are cursed if we pin our hopes on people. People will let us down. But when we make God, and God alone, our hope and confidence we will receive His blessing. Placing our trust in the God of hope will lead to our continual growth which, in turn will bring about an abundance of fruit in our lives; namely, "Love, joy, peace, patience, kindness, goodness, faithfulness, gentleness, and self-control" (Gal. 5:22–23, NIV).

In his letter to believers in Rome, the apostle Paul outlined the foundations of the Christian faith. He included a prayer that applied not just to Roman Christians, but to believers today as well: "I pray that God, the source of hope, will fill you completely with joy and peace because you trust in him. Then you will overflow with confident hope through the power of the Holy Spirit" (Rom. 15:13, NLT).

I like the phrase used in the King James Version of this text: *abounding in hope.* To *abound* is to teem, to overflow, to be abundantly filled or richly supplied. Our Heavenly Father desires that we not simply be somewhat hopeful in our outlook on life, but that we are filled to overflowing with hope.

Our Heavenly Father does not promise that only good things will happen to His kids. Our hope comes from His promise that whatever happens—good or bad—will be for our benefit. There are three things adversity does in the lives of God's children that can bring us hope:

1. It helps us to grow.
2. It helps us to help others.
3. It helps us to keep our eyes on Heaven.

Adversity Helps Us Grow

Here's the bottom line when it comes to getting on top when things turn our lives upside down: if we expect adversity and embrace it, we will be able to endure it. In the hands of God, endurance is crafted into personal, spiritual growth. The apostle Peter couldn't have said it more clearly: "Dear friends, don't be surprised at the fiery trials you are going through, as if something strange were happening to you. Instead, be very glad—because these trials will make you partners with Christ in His suffering, and afterward you will have the wonderful joy of sharing His glory when it is displayed to all the world" (1 Pet. 4:12–13, NLT).

Suffering leads to hope. It is in times of trouble that our Heavenly Father can do His best work in us. We don't learn how to persevere and become strong in times of smooth sailing; rather, it is in times when the waves are crashing, when our sails are tattered, and land is nowhere in sight that meaningful growth takes place.

Since God takes His role as Father seriously, He is all about helping His kids grow. We shouldn't then be surprised when difficulties arise. Adversity is a catalyst that triggers the spiritual growth needed to carry out God's grand plan for our lives. Satan would have us believe that God must not love us very much if He gives us so much heartache to deal with. But there is hope in knowing our Heavenly Father uses painful experiences in our lives to draw us into His loving arms so that He can nurture, strengthen, and equip us to do the work which Ephesians 2:10 tells us He has "prepared in advance for us to do."

It is said that when a mother eagle builds her nest, her supplies include rocks, thorns, and pieces of broken branches. Just before she lays her eggs, she puts down a protective padding of feathers, fur, and other soft materials. This blanket provides protection for the eggs and, once they're hatched, comfort for her young. The nest is so comfortable, in fact, that when the eaglets are old enough to fly, they are reluctant to leave.

At this point the mother eagle begins to stir up the nest, ripping out the lining and exposing the sharp rocks and branches beneath. The nest becomes uncomfortable for the eaglets and forces them to jump out and fly, which is their first step toward becoming the strong, majestic birds their Creator made them to be.

Has God stirred up your nest? Has he allowed discomfort in your life? Perhaps it is to move you to take a step you otherwise wouldn't take—a step that will make you stronger and help you to grow so that you can become the person He created you to be.

People who appear to have no problems just do a better job of hiding them.

Once we've come to expect adversity in our lives, we must learn how to embrace it. We're all wounded. It's part of our humanness. People who appear to have no problems just do a better job of hiding them. Embracing our woundedness cannot happen without having hope in a Heavenly Father who "causes everything to work together for the good of those who love [Him] and are called according to his purpose for them" (Rom. 8:18, NLT).

If we are driven by God our heartaches will not be roadblocks but highways to hope and healing. God's Word encourages us: "So be truly glad! There is wonderful joy ahead, even though it is necessary for you to endure many trials for a while. These trials are only to test your faith, to show that it is strong and pure. It is being tested as fire tests and purifies gold—and your faith is far more precious to God then mere gold. So if your faith remains strong after being tried by fiery trials, it will bring you much praise and glory and honor on the day when Jesus Christ is revealed to the whole world" (1 Pet. 1:6-7 NLT).

> **If we are driven by God our heartaches will not be roadblocks but highways to hope and healing.**

The devil seeks to destroy our faith in times of adversity. The Heavenly Father uses suffering to strengthen our resolve.

When our earthly fathers let us down, we can have hope that our Heavenly Father will lift us up. When even our brothers and sisters don't understand us, we can have hope that our Heavenly Father does. When our circumstances don't change and we wonder if we can go on, we can have hope that our Heavenly Father will see us through. We find hope in the bold words of Philippians 4:13: "I can do all things through Christ who strengthens me" (NKJV). Our Heavenly Father is a God of hope.

In Appreciation of Adversity

Statues are usually modeled after heroes, not villains. But that is not the case with the monument that graces the business district in the small town of Enterprise, Alabama. In the early 1900s, Enterprise was a thriving farm community thanks to an annually abundant cotton crop. That was before a pesky beetle known as the boll weevil made its first appearance there. In just three years, the ravenous insects had completely wiped out the fields of many farmers. Out of desperation, some of the farmers decided to try growing peanuts in the ravaged fields. That decision was a turning point for the town of Enterprise. The prosperity brought about by the peanut harvest was greater than the farmers had ever experienced growing cotton. The infestation of boll weevils, initially seen as devastating, turned out to be blessing in disguise.

In December of 1919, the people of the town dedicated a monument that said: "In profound appreciation of the Boll Weevil and what it has done as the herald of prosperity."

God has a divine purpose for every problem we face. We may not understand it at the time, but we can be assured that it's part of His plan. His intent is not to destroy us. His desire is that we grow. Jesus clarified, "The thief's purpose is to steal and kill and destroy. My purpose is to give life in all its fullness" (John 10:10, NLT).

Expect adversity. Embrace it. Endure it as part of our Heavenly Father's plan to help us grow in the fullness of life. As we plow through life we will come across many tough rows that we need to hoe. But if we remain diligent in our desire to grow in God's goodness, we will yield an abundant harvest. And it is a harvest that is meant to be shared.

Adversity Helps Us to Help Others

Experiencing trials not only helps us to grow, it helps us to help others to grow. It is said that adversity is life's greatest teacher. No students retain more knowledge than those who attend the School of Hard Knocks. Enduring the agony of a father's abandonment, the disappointment of divorce, the sorrow of sexual abuse, or the desolation of death doesn't just shape our thinking, it shapes our character.

When we face these tests and place our hope and trust in a Teacher whose objective is to make us prosper and give us hope, we can be assured that we will pass with flying colors. We will find our name on God's honor roll, credited with a stronger faith, a softer heart, and a resilient spirit. We will then be prepared to go out and make a difference in this world. Under God's tutelage, adversity can teach lessons that will serve us well in becoming better parents, better spouses, better coworkers, and better friends.

Persevering in tough times is not only meant to benefit us; we are to use what we have learned to bless those around us. We must share what we have learned. We must become teachers.

The apostle Paul explains it this way: "God is our merciful Father and the source of all comfort. He comforts us in all our troubles so that we can comfort others. When they are troubled, we will be able to give them the same comfort God has given us. For the more we suffer for Christ, the more God will shower us with his comfort through Christ. Even when we are weighed down with troubles, it is for your comfort and salvation! For when we ourselves are comforted, we will certainly comfort you. Then you can patiently endure the same things we suffer. We are confident that as you share in our sufferings, you will also share in the comfort God gives us" (2 Cor. 1:3b–7, NLT).

As we learn more about the hope and healing our Heavenly Father offers in times of adversity, we are better equipped to share our faith with others. God nudges us to "Always be prepared to give an answer to everyone who asks you to give the reason for the hope that you have" (1 Pet. 3:15, NLT). If we have in our hearts the hope of the Heavenly Father we must know this: All around us are people who need what we have.

If we have in our hearts the hope of the Heavenly Father we must know this: All around us are people who need what we have.

We all need hope.

Adversity Helps Us to Keep Our Eyes on Heaven

Most of us are familiar with the words of the Serenity Prayer: *God grant me the serenity to accept the things I cannot change; courage to change the things I can; and wisdom to know the difference.* These words, written by Reinhold Niebur some seventy years ago, have been adopted by Alcoholics Anonymous and many other twelve-step groups. They have been printed in books and on book markers, featured on posters and billboards, and cross-stitched on wall hangings. Niebur's words have been committed to memory by many a struggling soul.

What many people outside the recovery community don't know is that there is more to the prayer. The "Amen" comes later. The less quoted second part of the prayer speaks of eternity. The author's intent was to bring us from the serenity of surrender to the hope of heaven. To keep it in context, it is best that both parts be read together: *God grant me the serenity to accept the things I cannot change; courage to change the things I can; and wisdom to know the difference. Living one day at a time; enjoying one moment at a time; accepting hardships as the pathway to peace; taking, as He did, this sinful world as it is, not as I would have it; trusting that He will make all things rights if I surrender to His will; that I may be reasonably happy in this life and supremely happy with Him forever in the next. Amen.*

In its entirety, the Serenity Prayer reminds us that we must place our hope in God to make right what is wrong. That may not happen in this world, but it most certainly will in the next.

Our problems in this life may be overwhelming, but our Heavenly Father promises a happy ending to all who have hope in Him.

Our problems in this life may be overwhelming, but our Heavenly Father promises a happy ending to all who have hope in Him. The Bible promises, "Our present troubles are quite small and won't last very long. Yet, they produce for us an immeasurably great glory that will last forever! So we don't look at the troubles we can see right now; rather, we look forward to what we have not yet seen. For the troubles we see will soon be over, but the joys to come will last forever" (2 Cor. 4: 17–18, NLT).

We live in a world that is heartless and hateful, characteristics that are glaringly more pronounced by fatherlessness than many would like to believe. We can't expect that to change any time soon. The Bible warns us that people will become more and more selfish, disobedient, abusive, unforgiving, slanderous, and loveless (see

2 Timothy 3:1–7). Yet we have hope, despite that gloomy forecast, because the Bible also predicts with one hundred percent certainty that Jesus will one day return to earth, gather all who believe, and take us to live with Him and our Father in Heaven, where we will experience perfect peace and rest. Heaven is a place where the God of hope will wipe away every tear, where every wrong will be made right, where every sorrow will be turned to joy, where everyone who believes will experience life the way our Heavenly Father intended— in loving, intimate relationship with Him.

The hope of a perfect, peaceful, pain-free future makes today's problems easier to endure. That future is available to all who believe. In his book, *He Chose the Nails*, Max Lucado writes, "Any injustice in this life is offset by the honor of choosing our destiny in the next."

Some time ago I was having a conversation about heaven with a man from my church who was a former Greek professor at Moody Bible Institute. I asked him, "What is the most common misconception there is today about heaven?"

> **The hope of a perfect, peaceful, pain-free future makes today's problems easier to endure.**

His answer was so immediate I could barely finish the question: "That everybody goes there."

All of us want to believe that we go to a better place when we die. Religion offers all kinds of formulas to follow to get us there. Yet the Bible couldn't be clearer. Jesus said, "I am the way and the truth and the life. No one comes to the Father except through me" (John 14:6, NIV).

The apostle Peter reiterated that truth and could barely contain himself when he wrote, "Praise be to the God and Father of our Lord Jesus Christ! In His great mercy he has given us new birth into a living hope through the resurrection of Jesus Christ from the dead, and into an inheritance that can never perish, spoil or fade." Then Peter issued the promise: "This inheritance is kept in heaven for you" (1 Pet. 1:3–4, NIV).

To hope is to live in confident expectation that God, our Heavenly Father, will do what He says He will do. We can believe that He will. He is a Father we can trust. He is a Father who will never leave us and who will always love us. He is a Father who protects us and wants us to prosper. He is a Father who wants to hold us, encourage us, and spend time with us. He is a Father who is pleased with us; who suffers with us. He is hope to the hopeless. He is a Father to the fatherless.

Search for Him until you find Him. He has what you're looking for.

SOURCES

Chapter One: **When You Hear the Word** *Father*

[1] Ronald P. Rohner and Robert A. Veneziano, "The Importance of Father Love: History and Contemporary Evidence," *Review of General Psychology* 5, no. 4 (December 2001).

[2] Henry B. Biller, *Fathers and Families: Paternal Factors in Child Development* (Westport, CT: Auburn House, 1993).

[3] National Fatherhood Initiative, 2004.

[4] Marsha Kline Pruett, Tamra Y. Williams, Glendessa Insabella, and Todd D. Little, "Family and Legal Indicators of Child Adjustment to Divorce among Families with Young Children," *Journal of Family Psychology* 17 (June 2003): 169–80.

[5] Sim, Hee-Og and Sam Vuchinich, "The Declining Effects of Family Stressors on Antisocial Behavior from Childhood to Adolescence and Early Adulthood," *Journal of Family Issues* 17 (1996): 408–27.

[6] Steve Biddulph, *Raising Boys: Why Boys Are Different—And How to Help Them Become Happy and Well-Balanced Men* (Berkeley, CA: Celestial Arts, 2004).

[7] National Center for Fathering, Partnership for Family Involvement in Education, "A Call to Commitment: Fathers' Involvement in Children's Learning," June 2000.

Chapter Two: **A Father We Can Trust**

[8] Joseph M. Scriven, "What a Friend We Have in Jesus," 1855

[9] © 2001 worshiptogether.comm Songs (ASCAP) sixsteps Music (ASCAP) (adm. at EMICMGPublishing.com) All rights reserved. Used by permission.

Chapter Three: **A Father Who Will Never Leave Us**

[10] Rose M. Kreider and Jason Fields, *Living Arrangements of Children*, 2001. Current Population Reports, P70-104, Table 1, Washington, DC: US Census Bureau, 2005.

Chapter Five: **A Father Who Protects Us**

[11] Francis Chan, "God is Strong," in *What is God Really Like?*, p.11, ed. Craig Groeschel (Grand Rapids, MI: Zondervan, 2010).

Chapter Seven: **A Father Who Wants to Hold Us**

[12] Dr. Kenneth Condrell, Value Options, an Achieve Solutions website,

[13] H.F. Harlow, R.O. Dodsworth, and M.K.Harlow, "Total Social Isolation in Monkeys," *Proceedings of the National Academy of Sciences USA* 54, no. 1 (July 1965).

[14] EVERYTHING I OWN, Written by: David Gates, © 1972 Sony/ATV Music Publishing LLC. All rights administered by Sony/ATV Music Publishing LLC, 8 Music Square West, Nashville, TN 37203. All rights reserved. Used by permission.

Chapter Eight: A Father Who Encourages Us

[15] Helen Mrosla, © Shippensburg University. (Originally appeared in *Proteus: A Journal of* Ideas, Spring 1991.)

Chapter Ten: A Father Who is Please With Us

[16] Dr. Janet G. Woititz, *Adult Children of Alcoholics - the Expanded Edition,* © 1983, 1990.

Chapter Eleven: A Father Who Suffers With Us

[17] Dr. Myron J. Taylor, © 2002, from his message *The God Who Suffers With Us*

Visit

* to **read Dan's blog**

* to **find inspiration and encouragement**

* to **book Dan to speak** at your church, community, or school event

In addition to individual messages, Dan offers
Finding Father's Love Events in a number of formats.
(half-day workshops; full-day seminars; weekend
men's, women's, couples, and youth retreats)

All of Dan's messages are geared toward those seeking to deepen their
relationship with a Heavenly Father who longs to lavish His
love, healing, and grace on His children.